The
Parowan Gap

NATURE'S PERFECT OBSERVATORY

Sun, Moon, Venus, Polaris, and Constellations
An Introductory Interpretive Guide

By

V. Garth Norman

Petroglyph Drawings
by

Lance Harding

CFI
Springville, UT

The
Parowan Gap

NATURE'S PERFECT OBSERVATORY

Sun, Moon, Venus, Polaris, and Constellations

A Self-Guided Tour Book

By
V. Garth Norman

Petroglyph Drawings by
Lance Harding

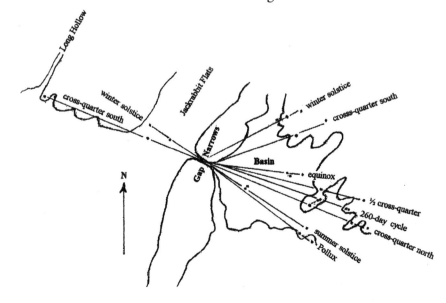

ISBN 13: 978-1-55517-995-3
ISBN 10: 1-55517-995-9

Published by CFI, an imprint of Cedar Fort, Inc.
2373 W. 700 S., Springville, UT, 84663
Distributed by Cedar Fort, Inc., www.cedarfort.com

LIBRARY OF CONGRESS CATALOGING-IN-PUBLICATION DATA

Norman, V. Garth.
  The Parowan Gap - nature's perfect observatory : an introductory interpretive guide / written by V. Garth Norman ; illustrated by Lance Harding.
    p. cm.
  Includes bibliographical references.
  ISBN-13: 978-1-55517-995-3
  1. Indians of North America--Utah--Parowan Gap--Antiquities. 2. Indian astronomy--Utah--Parowan Gap. 3. Indian calendar--Utah--Parowan Gap. 4. Archaeoastronomy--Utah--Parowan Gap. 5. Petroglyphs--Utah--Parowan Gap. 6. Parowan Gap (Utah)--Antiquities. I. Title.

  E78.U55N67 2007
  979.2'47--dc22

                              2006033625

Cover design by Nicole Williams
Cover design © 2007 by Lyle Mortimer
Printed in the United States of America

10 9 8 7 6 5 4 3 2 1

Printed on acid-free paper

Dedication

Dedicated to the preservation enrichment of the Parowan Gap for this and future generations.

In honor of our Native American friends and their ancestors who continue to show us the path of life is close to nature.

> We feel strongly, from the Hopi side, that the Anasazi, as well as other Puebloan classified cultures—like the Fremont farther north. . . . are in fact ancestral Hopi People . . . I think very important to the Hopi way of interpreting the presence of ancestral Hopi's here in this area is the interpretation of rock art. . . We should be proud that we hold some of the richest archaeological information, right here in the Southwest. And we're all in this together. The heritage that archaeology reveals is your heritage as well as mine.
>
> Leigh Jenkins, Cultural Preservation Officer of the Hopi Tribe (Widdison, 1991: 32)

Parowan Gap Narrows and Basin, looking northwest

Parowan Gap in Southwestern Utah is perhaps the most concentrated collection of Ancient Native American petroglyphs in the West with over 90 panels and 1,500 figures. It is heavily visited and locally famous for its many intriguing petroglyphs that, until now, have been an unsolved mystery.

Preface

The Parowan Gap, famous for its abundant rock art, is yielding its ancient secrets. Long regarded as undecipherable doodling, this fascinating pictographic "writing" can now be recognized as a rich archive recording the ancient history and beliefs of Utah's early inhabitants going back at least 5,000 years.

Archaeologist V. Garth Norman, Director of ARCON, Inc. (Archaeological Research Consultants), started the Parowan Gap Archaeology Project in 1993 with BLM cooperation. He was to excavate a cave shelter in the Gap and record petroglyphs found in the cave and at the Gap to study the site's cultural history. It soon became evident that the Gap pass was a sacred center of enormous importance that needed to be surveyed, recorded, and studied in detail to identify and preserve the rich cultural heritage remains that were gradually disappearing due to the impact of erosion, traffic, and vandalism.

An expanded project developed with a skilled staff and with the cooperation of Parowan City, Iron County, and other concerned private and governmental agencies, including the Paiute Tribe of southern Utah. The major fieldwork phase was accomplished with the help of a Federal Highways grant to Parowan City for a consulting contract with ARCON that funded a year's work in 1996–97. ARCON, Baseline Data, and Lamoreaux McLendon Associates Engineers funded final reports for a preservation enhancement design study.

Norman, the principal investigator of ARCON's Parowan Gap Archaeology Project (1993–2003), broke a code to reading rock art through integrating extensive data from field survey, excavation, recording rock art, remote sites comparison, archaeoastronomy, and ethnography (Native American traditions).

Lance Harding and Joel Clements assisted Garth Norman in the on-going field research documentation of observatory sites through 2005.

The massive wilderness temple center and calendar observatory at the Gap, which was discovered by Norman, reveals a far more sophisticated Parowan Fremont culture than previously known, with distant trade contacts to Mesoamerica.

The most surprising discovery was the Mesoamerican sacred 260–day calendar at the core of a sophisticated Fremont lunar-solar calendar recorded in the petroglyphs and observatory. The origin of this ritual calendar is believed to come from cultural exchange associated with turquoise trade from mines in northern Nevada with central Mexico, routed through Baker, Nevada, and Parowan Valley during the Post Classic Toltec period in Mexico, which coincides with the Parowan Fremont age (A.D. 700–1250).

This book, published in a self-guided tour format, includes the following Gap Project discoveries:

- Interdisciplinary archaeology project breaks code to rock art interpretation.
- Excavation of cosmic ritual cave identifies 5,000 years of rock art cultural history.
- Descriptive interpretive archiving of over 1,500 petroglyphs (92 panels).
- Decoded first complex calendar system in North America in petroglyphs with dates fixed by solar shadow markers and over thirty-two horizon observatory stations.
- Mesoamerican culture tie in discovery of 105/260-day sacred calendar involved with possible turquoise trade.
- Natural Fremont temple center spans 3.5 miles with sacred topography oriented to sun, moon, and star cycles.

Many of the author's rock art writing interpretations at the Gap are introduced for the first time in this book, which were made possible by the full archival record and integrated project data. They include the following:

- V-Lobe Gap Map—a master record of calendar and observatory events.
- April 29 New Year sunrise petroglyph markers.
- Sun-moon-Venus 8-year conjunction records on several panels.
- Lunar cycles pictographs with day tabulations.
- Fremont God focused from cave shelter panel to North Star on top of Narrows north peak.
- Horned-bird-serpent god tied to Soutwest and Mesoamerica.
- Trails Maps: Narrows south peak ascent; Gap basin terrain for observatory trails; Effigy maps cover 50 square miles of hunting-gathering trails across Red Hills; Sevier River and Sevier Lake map pictograph for geese migration.

Acknowledgments

The constant assistance and dedication of my wife made this book possible. We have learned together and marvel at the genius and patient wisdom of Native American people and their ancestors in keeping careful records of events in the heavens. The constant support and encouragement of the Ancient America Foundation staff has been invaluable. This book would not have been possible without the interest and editorial expertise of Lyle Mortimer and Lee Nelson and the staff at Cedar Fort, Inc. Steve Gibbons assisted with computer formatting and illustration graphics. I am indebted to Dr. C. Lance Harding for most petroglyph illustrations. My daughter, Rachel Williams, also helped with additional illustrations. Dr. John P. Pratt, astronomer, has been an instant resource for astronomy data assistance. Special thanks to Dixie Clifford, and Kirk and Shannon Magleby for assisting with editing and for friends Joel and Sylvia Clements, and Bob and Pat Jensen who have opened their homes to us during our many trips to the Parowan Gap.

The Parowan Gap project has been a coordinated effort between many concerned individuals, private and government agencies, including the Bureau of Land Management, Parowan City, Iron County Commission, Southern Paiute Tribe, Utah Division of State History, Utah Department of Transportation, and the Federal Highways Department that provided an ISTEA grant. As consultant to Parowan City for the contract, the many helpful city officials have been a pleasure to work with, including Rich Adams, John Bentley, Jim Burns, Nancy Dalton, Glenn Halterman, Jim Rasmussen, Jim Robins, Ronald Smith and especially Dennis Stowell, who after serving as Mayor became an Iron County Commissioner where he has extended support throughout this project.

BLM District Archaeologist Gardiner Dalley and BLM Environmental Specialist Bob Edwards have given time and effort to support this project. UDOT personnel helped with contract administration.

Asa Nielson and James Allison with Baseline data and staff helped with the excavation and report of the Gap cave shelter. Ben Lamoreaux with Lamoreaux McLendon Associates Consulting Engineers prepared detailed engineering construction design plans for the Gap. Nowell Morris assisted with contract preparation and archaeoastronomy tests of selected project sites.

Alex Shepherd, Chairman of the Southern Paiute Tribe, and Eleanor Tom, Cultural Resources Coordinator for the Cedar Band, coordinated Paiute Tribal interests.

Naturalist Martin Tyner, Southwest Wildlife Foundation, shared wildlife identifications with selected petroglyphs. Alan Walker also shared astute wildlife migration information. Amateur astronomer Joel Clements assisted with photography on key dates, recording sun and star positions. Gratitude is also expressed to many other colleagues, friends and family members, too numerous to mention whose encouragement and interest have aided this project.

Table of Contents ————————————

Interpretive Tour Guide Through the Gap Narrows

Introduction

Parowan Gap Archaeological Project, ARCON, Inc.

The Parowan Gap Narrows petroglyph site is perhaps the most visited and least understood prehistoric archaeological site in the state of Utah. I first visited this locally famous Indian rock art site while traveling with my family in 1973. The Utah tourist's road map said "Petroglyphs" on a dirt road 8 miles west of Parowan. Curiosity led us on a short side excursion. As we approached an imposing narrow split hog back mountain, I instinctively knew this was the place and would have been drawn here without the map. Cliffs, boulders and jagged outcrops on the steep talus slopes through a 300 meter mountain gap narrows are covered with hundreds of curious petroglyphs that accumulated here over perhaps millennia. What drew the people here to leave so many meticulously pecked figures? A two mile stretch of rock on through the Parowan Gap to the east valley lacks rock art. I felt the Narrows must have been a special sacred spot. It began to draw me in to explore the mystery.

The Gap Narrows is literally a gateway pass between the Great Basin Desert on the west and the Colorado Plateau mountains and valleys on the east. A brass plaque suggests a range of meanings related to hunting, travel and ritual, and of course a lot of "doodling" that cannot be interpreted. I did not believe that disclaimer, and would eventually prove it wrong. I was working at the time on a major archaeological project in southern Mexico, recording and deciphering pictographic rock art with the New World Archaeological Foundation's Izapa Project. My experience there was unwittingly preparing me for a future Gap project.

That trip in 1973 was my introduction to the Parowan Gap. I had no clue then that I would return two decades later to conduct a major archaeological project for interpretive preservation of Parowan Gap petroglyphs and related sites in the area to enhance the visitor's experience and stem vandalism. This project has been on the BLM's development priority list for many years. Perhaps no other major archaeology site in Utah today is at greater risk from vandalism and ongoing deterioration from visitation impacts. Numerous acts of vandalism of project sites occurred during our project.

The BLM has a saying that research brings understanding, understanding brings appreciation, and appreciation brings preservation. Due to the Gap's open access, the best hope for it's long term preservation is education and preservation development enhancement management. This book is dedicated to that end.

Research Design for Preservation Enhancement

The reader and public cannot understand and appreciate the scope and findings of the Parowan Gap Archaeological Project conducted by my consulting firm, ARCON without some understanding of the research process. This was a long and arduous journey of development and discovery that surmounted many obstacles. We moved from a virtual blank page over a ten year long project to major pioneering petroglyph sites research and decipherment that uncovered a remarkable wilderness temple center of the Parowan Fremont village culture that flourished here a thousand years ago. This discovery resulted from a major multi-disciplinary ten-year archaeological project from 1993 to 2003. Preliminary research and development planning took three years. Nine months of major field work data collection and analysis was accomplished from July 1996 through September 1997 under contract to Parowan City with UDOT management of a matching Federal Highways grant in cooperation with other concerned government agencies (BLM, SHPO, Southern Paiute Tribe).

Excavation, accurate recording of all rock art, and pedestrian archaeology survey of the Gap area for integrative sites were the three primary project tasks we would undertake. Another important specialized task for this project raised by preliminary studies and from my prior experience (Norman 1980), was an archaeo-astronomy survey of prospective calendar observatory sites (mostly rock cairns) on calendar cycle sight lines through the Narrows window to horizon sunrises and sunsets that we anticipated would correlate with calendar petroglyphs. Nal Morris (Solarnetics, Inc.) assisted with theodolite computer plots assigned from selected project survey sites of potential astronomical significance. None had been identified prior to our project. We would confirm the basic calendar system with Morris' assistance before he terminated in January 1998. I went on to confirm more than double the observatory inventory with onsite date observations of over 30 sites.

The second half of the project with the follow up field work, analysis and final reports preparation was funded privately by ARCON and associates and was completed in 2002. The success of this project resulted from ARCON's dedicated professional staff and their willingness to sacrifice to preserve the rich cultural heritage treasure at the Parowan Gap.

This brief outline of ARCON's multi-disciplinary archaeological research approach illustrates the work scope required for the Project's success. Work tasks centered on comprehensive rock art recording and analysis. Success in research interpretation of the rock art resulted from fully integrated analysis of rock art with other archaeology sites data that uncovered a calendar key to decipherment. Once that threshold was crossed, discoveries came at almost every turn. Overlapping collateral discoveries include:

- Two or more observatory stations for every key calendar date.
- Numic Indian traditional calendar system correlation.
- Petroglyph calendar shadow marker correlations with cairn observatory dates.
- A petroglyph calendar map of the major observatory system.
- The petroglyph map permitted a full disclosure of the entire calendar system with dates.
- A 105–260-day almanac fixed near the summer season cross-quarters (August 12 to April 29).
- Ritual calendar and observatory interactions with the cave shelter.

The extensive concentration of rock art in a distinctive style limited to the Gap Narrows became a huge attraction to me for integrated study. It would require tedious work to make an accurate record of nearly a hundred petroglyph panels and over 1,500 figures, many very weathered, to complete an accurate archival record for ongoing research. I had been successful with a similar project at Izapa, Mexico, so felt equal to the challenge here, given the opportunity and funding. Photo tracing drawings were completed by art historian Lance Harding with final field inspections and correlations by the author.

The cave shelter excavation inside the Narrows with a large half buried rock art panel and potential for deep occupational stratigraphy was also a big attraction for helping define the cultural history related to petroglyphs at the Gap. A successful excavation and report would be completed with subcontract assistance of Baseline Data, Inc.

In the final analysis, 31 observatory station sightings and 9 petroglyph calendar shadow markers produced the empirical data needed to confirm a massive wilderness temple center and calendar observatory at the Gap, which extended over a four mile distance through and beyond the full Parowan Gap pass, and encompassed nearly a square mile basin with the Narrows (see Astronomy Section).

Other research design tasks included a records search of prior research, comparative study of selected remote sites in Utah and Nevada, and ethnographic research of Indian traditions as a resource for interpretation. Comprehensive data collection from these seven tasks proved essential to getting culturally integrated, empirical data for objective interpretation. This work backed development of a preservation interpretive enhancement design plan with engineering construction plans completed by Lamoreaux Engineering under sub-contract to ARCON for future Phase 2 construction, which successfully completed ARCON's Gap Project contract deliverables to UDOT and BLM in 2002 for Parowan City and Iron County.

Perhaps no other major archaeology site in Utah today is at greater risk from vandalism and ongoing deterioration from visitation impacts. Due to its open accessible vulnerability, my hope for long range preservation is education shared in this book which can be a guide to stop visitors from vandalizing and desecrating this Native American sacred space. Extensive vandalism has brought forth nothing but destruction to parts of this ancient observatory. Long-term preservation depends on the character of each individual to work together as visitors, on a watchful public, and on enhancement development.

> *The Earth does not belong to us,*
> *We belong to the earth.*
>
> *Chief Seattle, 1854*

Native Americans
Mexico to Parowan Experience

I experienced my first sunrise hierophany at the ancient temple ruins of Izapa (ca. 300 B.C.) in southern Mexico on the June 21 summer solstice in 1978. My wife, Cheryl, and I traveled to this jungle ruin to view the sunrise on the distant Tajumulco volcanic peak standing in front of a monument that was anciently positioned toward the mountain for this sunrise date. I had discovered that numerous Izapa monuments had been placed in the temple's plazas to align with sunrises on the eastern mountain horizon (Norman 1980).

Fig. 1:1—Izapa Stela 9,
Oriented to Summer Solstice Sunrise

Cheryl and I stood in front of a 6.5 foot monument (Stela 9) that depicts a sun god rising with a human on his back into the heavens. As the sun glow intensified on the mountain, the first gleam of sunlight visually shot a light shaft to the monument (Fig 1:1) that gave us the distinct impression that the sun god depicted on the carving was rising with the summer solstice sun at its northern extreme into the heavens, a reflection of highland Maya tradition.

I would later discover that this temple center was located here to view the Venus rise at its northern standstill directly over the Tajumulco peak. This was a first discovery in Mesoamerican archaeology.

Archaeology, astronomy and ethnology were combined to make this exciting Izapa rock art discovery that I would see repeated many times over the next two decades in my explorations of rock art sites in Mexico, the Southwest and Great Basin, climaxing with the discoveries at the Parowan Gap.

About the same time I was researching astronomy in Mexico, I started looking for solar interactions with petroglyphs during my archaeology field work in Utah where I was able to make the first discoveries. At Dry Fork in the Uintah Basin I watched the sunrise in a prominent notch across a draw from a petroglyph panel that pictures the event with a glyph containing 12 dots (a year). In the 1980s I witnessed similar events on the Green River, the Book Cliffs, at Nine Mile Canyon and in Douglas Creek south of Rangely, Colorado. From these experiences my life's work in archaeology grew to emphasize rock art research and the ancient astronomy of the American West.

Southwest—"Think Indian"

Living in balance with nature and honoring it is a way of life for tribal Native Americans and their ancestors. Some years ago a leading American archaeologist confirmed a research approach I tried to follow while working as an educator with Native American Tribes on reservations in Nevada, Arizona and New Mexico (1965–1976) before becoming a full-time archaeologist. He said that to interpret the true picture of the past we must learn to "think Indian," to try and see through the eyes of the people we study.

When our family lived at Window Rock, Arizona in the 1970s, we traveled on occasion around the Four Corners area visiting Anasazi ruins. The picturesque cliff dwellings at Canyon de Chelly was one of our favorite places. We drove west to the Hopi Mesa area to watch life cycle ceremonial dances and learn of the Hopi culture. We also visited the Zuni in New Mexico and studied their traditional culture. Chaco Canyon was full of intrigue with its massive ruins that have extensive astronomical orientations. We marveled at the dramatic feat of architectural achievement in cliff dwellings at Mesa Verde in Colorado.

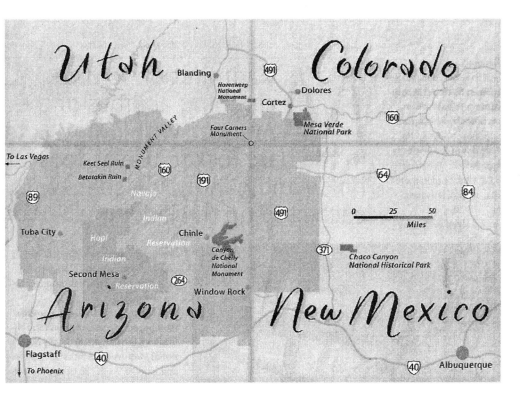

Fig. 1:2 (Toll 2005: 43)

Reading about Southwest cultures became a favorite pastime on these trips. Two of our favorite books on these memorable excursions were *The Book of the Hopi* (Frank Waters 1963) and *Laughing Boy* (Oliver LaFarge 1957).

As we traveled north to Utah and drove through Parowan we became acquainted with the ancient Fremont villages in this area. Later during the Parowan Gap research, I observed how the Fremont villages at Parowan, Paragonah and Summit were aligned to winter solstice sunset and equinox sunrises and sunsets which led me to take a closer look. The plaza mounds in the Paragonah village align with winter solstice sunrise. This widespread Mesoamerican tradition is also prevalent at Chaco Canyon. Mesoamerican cultural contact with the Southwest is a well established field of study that has been neglected in Fremont archaeology until now with the Parowan Gap archaeological project. The Parowan and Paragonah village sites have been excavated by the University of Utah and UCLA but results are not well known locally.

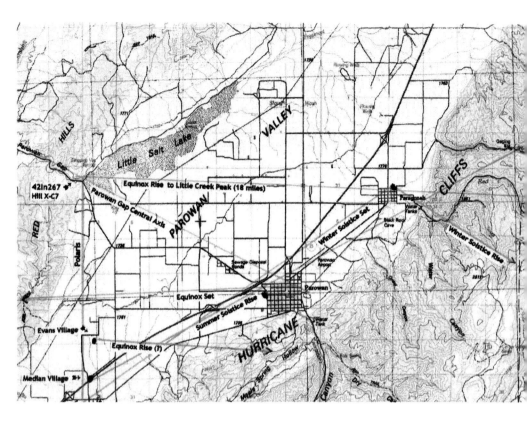

Fig. 1:3 (Norman 2002)
Parowan Valley—Fremont Village Sites at Paragonah,
Parowan, Summit/Midian, and Evans Mounds

Research by Local Explorers

A 20th century explorer, LaVan Martineau, was employed by the Paiute Tribe to help record and interpret petroglyphs on the Clear Creek project (Shepherd and Martineau 1985) and Quail Creek project (Parashonts, Shepherd, Martineau, and Benn 1985). Martineau's open scholarly inquiry was demonstrated by his conclusion that most of these petroglyphs were of earlier Fremont origin, mostly related to the Southwest Anasazi, and had limited but identifiable Paiute connections. Martineau's many contributions to interpret and preserve rock art are of much value to continuing research.

While the Paiute Tribe has territorial jurisdiction today, there is evidence that other peoples, including the Ute and Hopi, earlier ranged in this area, as indicated by Ute Chief Wakara's knowledge of the Gap as a sacred site that he related to early pioneers. The Parowan Fremont village culture's relation to the greater Southwest culture has become common knowledge. Because the Paiutes were a nomadic culture, some

Paiute elders regard archaeological sites in Southwestern Utah with permanent type dwellings as the ruins of the Anasazi or Hopi who came into this area (eg. Parashonts and Shepherd, 1985: Part 4, Yetta Jake Interview).

A Paiute legend relates how a scouting party crossed the west desert in search of a cave in a mountain where the first Paiute ancestors emerged from the underworld (Palmer 1978: 14–20). Upon reaching a mountain, they met the god Shinob (in a small cave opening) who showed them a rock pinnacle high up that looked like an Indian, with a raised hand behind its head like an eagle feather; this was identified as an image of the creator god Tobats. From this image the men were directed to wear an eagle feather at the back of their heads so Tobats would bring them good luck (Palmer 1978: 14–20). The cave entrance they sought was above the pointing hand that could not be reached because it was high in the rocks. Was this Paiute legend adapted to the rock features at the Parowan Gap?

Another local explorer, Alva Matheson of Cedar City, was an avid student and friend of the Paiutes. In his *Indian Stories and Legends* he recorded interviews with them. The Paiutes told him that the large V-lobe glyph was "a map and calendar of travels" (Matheson 1990). They also shared their legends of the god Tobats and showed him the Tobats god "face" on the south cliff of the Gap Narrows where the rock formations seem to form a large side view of a human forehead-nose-mouth. Matheson recorded many petroglyphs and archaeology sites throughout the Iron County area.

A somewhat related Paiute tradition known locally, but not formally recorded and published, tells how the god Tobats while standing on the north peak of the Gap appeared and taught the Paiutes. Similar traditions of heavenly messengers appearing and giving instruction are widespread and cannot be attributed to any common origin.

Ancient Turquoise Trade Route

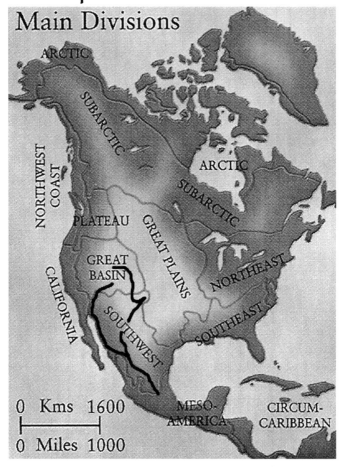

Fig. 1:4 (Jones and Molyneaux 2002: 15)
Bold lines added to indicate approximate turqoise trade routes.

Ancient cultural interaction between Southwest Pueblo-Anasazi and Mesoamerica is becoming well known. The extent and nature of the interaction is not so clear. Trade seems to have been the major avenue for cultural exchange. A trade network of particular interest to the Parowan Fremont in Parowan Valley and Baker, Nevada was the turquoise trade with Mexico from about A.D. 850 during Toltec through Aztec times. The northern most turquoise mine was near Elko, Nevada. Traders leaving the mine probably passed through Baker and Parowan Valley on a southern route through New Mexico and south into central Mexico. Trace analysis of ancient turquoise sources in Mexico and at Chaco Canyon, New Mexico shows that some turqoise came from northern Nevada mines (*Scientific American*, February 1992: 78–85, Harbottle and Weigand).

Fig. 1:5 (Norman 2002)

The Parowan Gap in southwestern Utah is in the Great Basin region of the western United States, as were the ancient Nevada turquoise mines. Riley (1986) described how early Spanish explorers were able to easily move along established trails and trade routes linking the Valley of Mexico and the Southwest. These early explorers moved north as easily on established trails into the Great Basin area.

We sometimes think today that ancient people didn't travel much without horses and automobiles. A Hopi boy (1968) at a boarding school in Nevada who was a marathon runner told me how he had run with his father in the deserts of Arizona chasing wild horses. They ran up to 80 miles in one day until one horse was so tired that they walked up and put a rope around his neck.

Timeline
(See Appendix Cultural Descriptions)

	Parowan Fremont	Southwest Pueblo	Central Mexico
A.D. 1850	Euro-American		
	Mormon Pioneer Settlement ————————		
A.D. 1700	Spanish Contact ———————		
A.D. 1680 (Aug. 13)		Pueblo Revolt Against Spanish Rule	
A.D. 1600	Spanish Exploration	Spanish Settlement at Sante Fe, NM	
A.D. 1521			Spanish Conquest
A.D. 1350	Numic (Ute, Paiute Shoshone)	Pueblo IV	
A.D. 1150		Pueblo III	
A.D. 1093	Aztec Contact		Aztec
A.D. 950	Toltec Contact	Pueblo II	
A.D. 800		Pueblo I	Toltec—Yucatan
A.D. 700	Parowan Fremont		Toltec rise
A.D. 600			Teotihuacan Decline
A.D. 500		Basketmaker III	
A.D. 250			Classic Maya
A.D. 100			Teotihuacan
A.D. 50		Basketmaker II	
		Basketmaker I (Pre-A.D. 50)	
500 B.C.			Early Maya
1000 B.C.	Late Archaic		
1500 B.C.			Olmec
2500 B.C.	Middle Archaic		
4500 B.C.	Early Archaic (Unknown)		

Ute Chief Wakara told the first white settlers who
entered Parowan Valley in 1850 that the Gap west
of Little Salt Lake is "God's own house."

Paiute Legends & Religious Traditions

**Fig. 2:1—Side view of Paiute god
Tobats (mouth open) on south Narrows cliffs**

Archaeological evidences indicate that native Paiute and other Numic speakers moved into the Colorado Plateau region after the Fremont hiatus around A.D. 1250. Paiute traditions speak of ancestral migrations, but they also believe their ancestors were among the earliest inhabitants here. After studying Paiute traditions and beliefs, I have found significant similarities with calendar petroglyphs which persuade me to accept both views (see Cave Shelter Discussion—Area G). There is also significant petroglyph evidence at the Gap to sustain the Hopi traditional belief that their ancestors also lived in Utah during the Fremont era. With local Paiute interest in antiquities in southwestern Utah, particular attention is given in this section to their traditions.

Measurement of Time

"It is of interest to note that time was the only thing for which the Pahutes [Paiutes] had a standard of measurement. . . . The day is divided into three parts; the night into one. A day and a night is called a 'sleep' " (Palmer 1978:113).

"The doorway or entrance to all Paiute dwellings faced the sunrise. Most members of a community would pray together at sunrise, noon and sunset," usually led by their chief (niavi). Throughout Paiute country, chiefs were expected to perform certain duties. One of the most important of these was the morning speech, during which the chief would announce plans for the day and exhort people to live in harmony with each other (Bunte and Franklin 1990: 35, 37–38).

"To divide the day, the sky is cut at the angle of the North Star. The east section is called 'ich-coot', which means the sun ascending or climbing. The center section is called 'ta-haut'tavi', meaning the sun overhead. The west section is called 'tavi-mum-wiski', meaning the sun descending or sinking. . . . One cycle of the moon, from new moon to new moon, is called 'mat-oit' or moon. Twelve moons is a year and is called a 'snow'. A snow is divided into four seasons of three moons each." (Palmer 1978: 113–118).

The Paiutes have names for 16 directions:

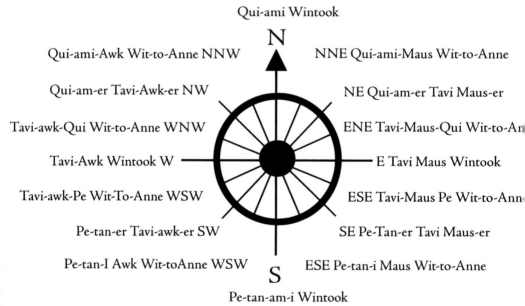

Qui-ami Wintook

N

Qui-ami-Awk Wit-to-Anne NNW   NNE Qui-ami-Maus Wit-to-Anne

Qui-am-er Tavi-Awk-er NW   NE Qui-am-er Tavi Maus-er

Tavi-awk-Qui Wit-to-Anne WNW   ENE Tavi-Maus-Qui Wit-to-An

Tavi-Awk Wintook W   E Tavi Maus Wintook

Tavi-awk-Pe Wit-To-Anne WSW   ESE Tavi-Maus Pe Wit-to-Ann

Pe-tan-er Tavi-awk-er SW   SE Pe-Tan-er Tavi Maus-er

Pe-tan-I Awk Wit-toAnne WSW   ESE Pe-tan-i Maus Wit-to-Anne

S

Pe-tan-am-i Wintook

Fig. 2.2 (Palmer 1978: 113)

Paiute Creation Legends

The Paiute gods Tobats and Shinob created the earth, sun, moon, stars, the seasons, land, water, plants, animals and human beings. Paiute astronomy is "hitched to the North Star. It alone is steadfast and constant" (Palmer 1978: 113). The precision sighting place at the Gap for seeing the North Star is near "Tobat's head" at the entrance of the south Cave Shelter looking on top of the north Gap peak where Polaris sits.

At some point in the remote past, Uto-Aztecan ancestors of Shoshone, Ute and Paiute tribes related a legend of the creation of time, which is reflected at the Gap. The animals held a council to decide how long the seasons should be. The birds recommended 4 seasons with three moons each to match their toes. This would balance the seasons so that summer heat would not be too long and winter cold not long enough to destroy life (Palmer 1978: 70). Today we see that the migratory birds keep the seasons in check in their annual flights recorded at the Gap (see Panel D7 depicting the white geese flight north in late February to usher in the spring season).

Paiute Religious Traditions

Paiute legends and religious traditions have identifiable connections with ancient calendar records at the Parowan Gap. "The religious life of the early Paiute revolved around two important types of ceremonies. One type was the life-cycle rituals, or rites of passage. . . . The three most important events in the life cycle of an individual were puberty, the birth of a first child, and death. All three were marked by special rites.

"The other important group of Paiute rites were those that honored the spirits of the natural world. [The Paiutes] prayed and conducted rituals to influence the spirits of nature and show their respect and gratitude to them. . . . There were many supernatural beings, but one was more powerful than all the others—The One Who Made The Earth. The sun was one visible manifestation of this spirit. The Paiute also associated the mythical heroes, Coyote and Wolf, with this powerful spirit, seeing the good and virtuous Wolf and the wicked and silly Coyote as two necessary sides of the same all-powerful creator" (Bunte and Franklin 1990: 39–42).

Food—Agriculture, Hunting and Gathering

In 1776 Dominguez and Escalante described the many Paiute communities that "farmed the fertile lands around springs and long rivers." These native peoples cultivated crops with "well-dug irrigation ditches . . . [and] the women primarily gathered wild berries and roots, while the men hunted wild game. During gathering or hunting expeditions they would pray to plants and animals before harvesting their resources. The Paiute thanked their quarry, asking it to be good food, or good medicine for them. Otherwise the plant or animal would not give its special power to the people or might prove difficult to find the next time it was needed" (Bunte and Franklin 1990: 27–33, 42).

"Pinenuts [a food staple] were blessed twice each year. In the spring when the cones were small, the people would go into the mountains and pray. In the fall, the pinenuts were harvested and the people would give thanks. The harvest of the pinenuts was also a time of courtship. People would gather together in camp and dance . . . Tuhva tzi buina. The word tuhva describes the pinenuts peeking forth from the cone as it opens up. If the word 'tuhva' is used, [a] song becomes a sunrise 'prayer' song and describes the sun peeking forth as the day opens. . . . When singing thanks after a good harvest and praying for another one, two people would throw pinenuts on the ground in a circle as a gesture of replenishment" (Trejo 1997: 4).

Family Relations

"Family relationships and marriage in Paiute society created ties that united each community and cemented alliances between communities. . . . Despite their many blood relationships, marriages were never with blood relatives. Families would travel great distances to participate in circle dances with distant tribes so their young people could meet and marry suitable mates. . . . If a young man danced four nights with the same partner and refused to let anyone cut in, the partners were considered married. Marriage has been an important institution for the Paiute people with infidelity and promiscuity punishable by death in the past" (Bunte and Franklin 1990: 39).

"Circle dance songs are about nature and everyday experiences and include humor which is considered as healing and sacred as anything else . . . Laughter is good medicine . . . One of the purposes of dance in the Paiute culture is to provide healing . . . All healing songs are prayer songs . . . 'Come and dance your sickness away, dance your heartache away' " (Trejo 1997: 3–4).

Fig. 2:3—Paiute Traditional Circle Dance—Cedar City
(Photo by author)

Three Ways the Ancients— "Measured Time"

The beauty of the Parowan Gap calendar is that we can track and identify the whole calendar system three different yet integrated ways:

1. **Cairns** (rock piles) were set in positions in the valleys on the east and west side of the Gap Narrows by the Fremont about a thousand years ago to watch sunrises and sunsets on specific calendar cycle dates .

2. **Number and Map Petroglyphs** were pecked on cliffs around the Gap Narrows to indicate day, month, season and year counts for moon, sun, and Venus star cycles with dots, lines, ladder circles, triangles, trees, combs, serpents, etc. Map migration glyphs tie into calendar counts. (Most are on strategic viewing and sighting rock cliffs).

3. **Shadow-Marker Petroglyphs** were pecked for strategic viewing and sighting on rock cliffs inside the Gap Narrows to record the same dates as the cairns.

Fig. 3:1
Cairn B1—Cross-Quarter

Fig. 3:2
Sunset viewed from B1

1. CAIRNS

Archaeo-astronomy is modern man's way of discovering how people in the past measured and recorded the sun, moon and star cycles in the heavens. At the Parowan Gap, observatory cairns (rock piles) were built by ancient astronomers in the valleys up to a mile on the east and west sides of the Gap Narrows cliffs. Each cairn is in a position for watching a sunrise or sunset on a specific calendar cycle date through the Gap Narrows such as Summer Solstice on June 21. (see Sun Cycle Chart.) Cairns also corre-late with petroglyph sun shadow calendar markers and with moon and sun cycle number petroglyphs.

The Last Calendar Station

In 1995, Lance Harding and I had exhausted our search for the basic cairn stations of the Gap calendar system. The winter solstice was the only position lacking a precise cairn. It was time to set our archaeology method aside and track the setting winter sol-stice sun the way the ancients did. We hiked to the top of the north peak on December 21, 1995, where winter solstice sunset could be seen from Cairn G3 but lacked the precision of the other cairns. We walked down slope to a spot where the setting sun was barely visible on the distant V–Gap horizon.

Over a thousand years ago Parowan calendar watchers had located equinox cairn E1 in this same way. As we watched, I was disappointed that there was no cairn rock pile. It had doubtless eroded away down the steep slope centuries ago, I thought. Lance pointed to a standing boulder about ten feet to our right. I moved to this upright boul-der (G1) just in time to see the last gleam of the winter solstice sun disappear where the distant horizon met the right slope of the Gap V. (Fig. 3:3)

Fig. 3:3—G1 Boulder, Winter
Solstice Sunset View

Fig. 3:4—G1 Boulder, Winter
Solstice Sunrise View

I can't describe the thrill of that moment discovering the ancient marker by using the ancient sky watchers method. To witness what had perhaps not been seen for 800 years transported me back in time and I seemed to touch the spirits of the ancestors. My respect deepened. I vowed not to fail in my quest to find and help preserve the rich truths and the cultural heritage left here.

The sun had entered its midwinter home. Sunrise the next day would signal the sun's rebirth in Southwest tradition, to begin life's return to mother earth with the sun's warmth. Where was the sun-rise marker? I noticed this same large boulder's flat face aligned east. My compass indicated it could be aligned with winter solstice sunrise!

The next morning, full of anticipation, we climbed to the proximity of our sunset watch the night before. I set up my tripod and camera by the boulder focused for the east rising sun. The sky was almost completely overcast, and we were cold. Magically, the sun burst on the eastern horizon in perfect alignment with the flat face of the sunset boulder where we stood the night before! Our ancestral predecessors were ingenious astronomers. The G1 winter solstice cairn boulder marks both winter solstice *sunrise* and *sunset*! This completed the cairn stations for the full base calendar system and further confirmed the dual summer solstice Cairns A1 and A2. (Fig. 3:3 and 3:4).

In the final analysis a total of seven cairn observatory stations were identified that have one or more backup cairns (totaling 25) to watch specific calendar sunsets on the horizon through the Gap Narrows.

After visiting the Gap on several solstice, equinox and cross-quarter dates to watch sunrises and sunsets, astronomer Dr. John Pratt agreed with my assessment that "this is a natural ancient Stone Henge observatory."

Puebloan calendar priests in the Southwest today still have observatory points for measuring time. The ancient Pueblo calendar system was based on the trained calendar priest being able to spot key dates by standing at a calendar shrine to watch the sun's rise or descent on a distant horizon feature. Puebloan calendar priests still use petroglyph shadow markers by spotting the sunlight shadow on key dates across a doorway, post, or through a window. The Gap Narrows is a natural "window" created by nature for watching sunrises and sunsets to measure time.

North-South Sun Transit

Five primary sun dates begin the year in the north at summer solstice sunset and move south in six months to winter solstice sunset. Because of the earth's tilt, the sun appears to reverse its path moving back north to summer solstice. This annual Sun Transit is observed through the Gap from cairn observatory stations east of the Gap Narrows to the west. These sunset movement patterns follow the diagram below—winter to summer solstice sunset observations move south (1-2-3-4-5), then back north from summer to winter solstice (5-4-3-2-1).

1.	Summer Solstice	June 21
2.	Summer Cross-Quarter	May 5 and August 5
3.	Equinox	September 20 and March 21
4.	Winter Cross-Quarter	November 5 and February 5
5.	Winter Solstice	December 21

1.
2.
3.
4.
5.

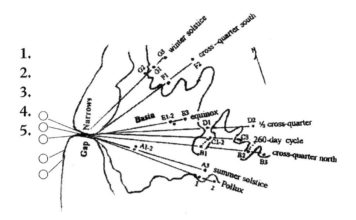

Fig. 3:5

Fig. 3:6

Parowan Gap Map of Cairn Positions

The Calendar Observatory Map on the previous page illustrates the location of cairns (rock piles) [1] positioned for ancient sky watchers to observe sunsets through the Gap Narrows on primary calendar cycle dates: June 21 and December 21 solstices, September 22 and March 22 equinoxes and cross-quarters between these. Also of importance are the five 260–105 day ancient Sacred Calendar Cairns at or near the cross-quarter positions. The following Solar Calendar Chart illustrates the relationship between these dates.

Summer Solstice	**June 21** Sunset Cairns A1, A2, and A3 are east by Narrows road. A1 sunset "slides" down the south cliff, illuminating the Tobats god face on the cliff. A2 and A3 sunset center in the Narrows. Summer to Winter Solstice = **182 days (½ year)**
Cross-Quarter	**Aug. 5** and **May 5** Sunset Cairns B1, B2 and B3 = **45 days (⅛ year)**
Sacred Calendar	**Apr. 29** and **Aug. 13** (260–105 day Ancient Calendar) Sunset Cairns B1, B2, C1, C2, and C3
½ Cross-Quarter	Sunset Cairns D1 and D2 = **22 days (¹⁄₁₆ year)**
Equinox	**Sept. 21–22** and **March 21–22** Cairns E1 and E2 = **91 days (¼ year)**
Winter Cross-Quarters	**Nov. 5** and **Feb. 5** Cairns F1 and F2 = **45 days (⅛ year)**
Winter Solstice	**December 21** Boulder G1 on the north hill slope appears to be on a parallel N–S line with the west ridges forming a bracket with the Summer Solstice Boulder A1 = **182 days (½ year)**

---

1. Criteria for identifying ancient cairns includes, (1) calendar system location, (2) precision astronomical positioning, (3) comparative topographic position, (4) proximity to and distinction from historic cairns [mineral exploration or USGS survey], (5) duplicate astronomical cairn function, (6) dual prehistoric/historic cairn function, (7) coded stone numbers, (8) surface artifact association, (9) erosion action relative age indicator, (10) test excavation for stone erosion deposition and subsurface deposits.

Observatory Cairns
Events Dates & Times

Note: Gradual day shifts occur thru the four-year leap-year cycle. Precision observations can vary slightly based on the original date set of an observatory cairn in the leap-year cycle.

Sunset Calendar Event	Date	Cycle	Station	Time
Winter End; Start Spring Season	Feb 5	Cross-Quarter	Cairns F1, F2	5:59 P.M.
Mid Spring	Mar 23	Vernal Equinox	Cairns E1, E2	6:44 P.M.
Birth; Start Summer Growth	Apr 29	105-Day Cycle	Cairns B1, B2, C1, C2, C3	8:05 P.M.
End Spring; Start Summer Season	May 6–7	Cross-Quarter	Cairns B1, B2	8:24 P.M.
Mid Summer (5-day observation)	June 20–21	Summer Solstice	Cairns A1, A2, A3	8:51 P.M.
Summer End; Start Autumn Season	Aug 4–5	Cross-Quarter	Cairns B1, B2	8:33 P.M.
First Fruits Harvest; Start Gestation	Aug 12	260-Day Cycle	Cairns B1, B2, C1, C2, C3	8:14 P.M.
½ Season	Aug 27	½ Cross-Quarter	Station D1	7:52 P.M.
Mid Fall	Sept 18–19	Autumn Equinox	Cairns E1, E2 (day lead)	7:31 P.M.
End Fall; Start Winter Season	Nov 4	Cross-Quarter	Cairns F1, F2	5:28 P.M.
Mid Winter	Dec 21–22	Winter Solstice	Boulder G1	Sunrise 8:40 A.M. Sunset 5:09 P.M.

Sunrise Calendar Event	Date	Cycle	Station	Time
Equinox Sunrise over East Peak	Mar 23 Sept 21–22			7:08 A.M. 7:53 A.M.
Gap Notch Sunrise; Start Winter Season	Nov 5	Cross-Quarter	Cairns I-1, I-2	7:19 A.M.
Gap Notch Sunrise; End Winter Season	Feb 5	Cross-Quarter	Cairns I-1, I-2	7:49 A.M.
Winter Solstice Approach Sunrise	Dec 5	Over Tobats Cave	Cairn H1	8:42 A.M.

Moon Cycle Eastern Horizon Event	Date	Cycle	Station	Time
19-Year Metonic Moon Rises at Summer Solstice	June 21–05	Full Moon	Moon Panel Slot	9:44 P.M.
	June 21–24	Full Moon	Moon Panel Slot	9:54 P.M.
	June 21–43	Full Moon	Moon Panel Slot	10:15 P.M.

Azimuth 131.7 to 132.4; Elevation 4.2 to 4.4

(Compiled from Morris 1998)

Venus Cycle Event

Northern Standstill sets in Gap from hill point south of Summer Solstice Cairn A3 (to be determined)

Venus-Sun 8-year, 2920-day Conjunction observations (to be determined)

2. GAP CALENDAR OBSERVATORY MAP

**Fig. 3:7—V–Gap Calendar Map and
Observatory Petroglyph Panel A7**

The large imposing V–Gap petroglyph that greets the visitor approaching the east entrance to the Narrows pass has impressed many to speculate that it could be a picture of the Narrows. When I overlaid my drawing of this petroglyph onto a photo of the Gap Narrows (as viewed from Cairn A3) the correlation became obvious. The length, angles and curves on the two arms are a nearly perfect match. The serpent trail down the right side maps the ridges of the east basin (Fig. 3:8). The trail arm off the bottom lobe represents the east basin with two rows of 5 dots as the prime observatory stations for the two halves of the year.

What more could we ask for? How about a full record-observatory stations map, sunsets map, and the entire calendar system recorded in one mammoth petroglyph panel. It is all here.

Serpent Trail Terrain Observatory

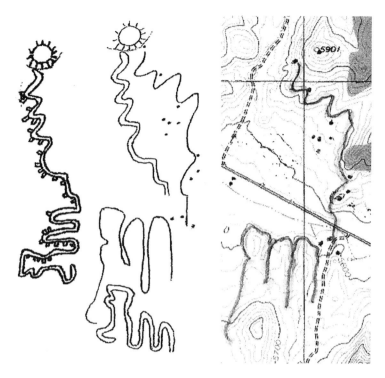

Fig. 3:8—Serpent Trail

There is a long meandering serpent trail along the right north arm of the V–Gap petroglyph that extends from a horizon sun down below the basin lobe. It starts at the top like a common serpent with 12 turns before its extended "tail". The "tail" was a pecked "add-on" extending around the lobe. My first impression was that this serpent "tail" is a terrain map of the east valley. A USGS topographic map (above) shows the ridges with almost the exact curves and turns of the serpent trail in the petroglyph.

So we have the terrain, but what about the observatory cairns along that terrain? Some tics on the serpent trail appear to match the observatory cairns, but we do not have an actual observatory trail, only the terrain map along that trail. However, 7 of the 11 observatory cairns are on the terrain map. Only those around equinox and summer solstice cairns are some distance from the hills. Rather than try to map the full observatory trail, the ancient scribe apparently chose to label it by placing 29 day tics along the serpent for a month to magnify the 12 turns as a label for a full year. The setting sun at the head of the serpent with 13 rays for the 13 new moons in a year clinches the case. And this big sun is where the real map takes off to the left.

Observatory Sunset Map

We can now go to the next level for an actual map of the observatory cairns, not in the basin cairns themselves, but in what is seen on the horizon. Notice how two rays of the sun at the head of the serpent trail flank an arm tic that is an extension of the horizon map between the two V–Gap arms. The so-called "ladder" below climbs through the Narrows on 6 steps and is a ladder only in the sense that it records the sun "climbing" the calendar clock ladder through its 6-month solar transit from winter solstice to summer solstice at the top. This picture may, in fact, be the origin of the familiar calendar ladder figures for recording months—so prevalent at the Gap.

Summer Solstice Sunset

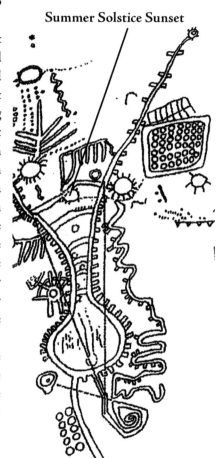

Each ladder step is the same horizon but at a different month or cycle point date recorded with its own small round sun. There are a total of 8 "sun" circles adjacent to these steps. Sunset positions vary at different stations depending on the view, with the sun in the center or at the right or left inside the Gap cliffs. When I plotted these sunsets in sequence and then rotated them against the petroglyph map, a perfect match results with the summer season at the top where the big sun setting under the horizon in the middle is summer solstice. The smaller double circle for two dates setting above against the right north cliff starts the summer growing season—the dates are April 29 for spring birth, and May 5—six days later in the comb overhead for summer cross-quarter.

We should note that the summer solstice also rests on a natural "horizon" ridge in the stone that continues to the right beneath the other large sun that is at the head of the serpent trail.

Fig. 3:9

Spiral at Base of V–Lobe

The spiral observatory trail for Cairn B2 east of the Narrows basin is mapped below the V–lobe and records both horizon sunsets against the side cliffs for summer cross-quarter (May 5–August 5) and the April 29 New Year date (August 12 return date) with the 6-day interval recorded on the big comb over the horizon setting sun. On a hunch, I sized and overlaid the spiral on the terrain map (Fig. 3:10 bottom), and found each turn of the spiral aligns with the observatory cairns between summer solstice and equinox. Fantastic as it may seem, this could be a map of that system.

We are now prepared to consider the full calendar system recorded in the V–Gap map in other sections (Sky Watchers, Panels A7, H, J). Where the sun, moon and Venus shine through their intermeshing cycles there is much to consider in the numbers and associated figures for deciphering the full calendar system.

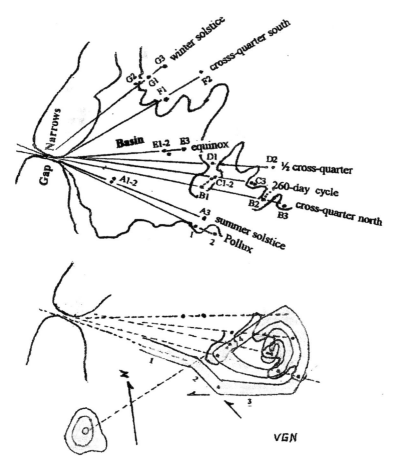

Fig. 3:10

Venus Glyph

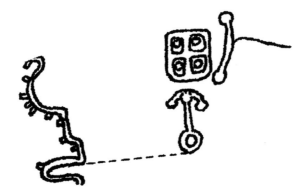

Fig. 3:11

A Venus note with respect to the observatory trail map deserves mention. My associate Nal Morris back-sighted a Venus azimuth from the narrows for a prospective Evening Star northern maximum standstill to a good observatory ridge point just south of the summer solstice Cairn A3. We examined a small cairn there with a wooden survey peg and concluded with no signs of erosion that it is a modern survey. We can only speculate if the surveyor gathered stones from a nearby eroded cluster left by an ancient astronomer. This kind of modern survey impact actually happened in 2004 which almost destroyed two of the sunset observatory cairns. The petroglyph map may help solve this mystery. The serpent "terrain trail" break where the right angle takes off to the lower south side of the basin (detached in figure) can be matched up with the ridge point in question by projecting the relative distances of the adjacent terrain on the north. We find that various relationships between separated figures on this and other panels were designed through sight-line pointers. The bottom spiral trail figure is especially detailed in this way. If we extend the south ridge line map at the right angle, it points right to a concentric circle on a figure that I had previously identified with Venus cycle observations. The solstice cairn tic also ties right to the 4-quarter seasons box alignment and its solstice-equinox markers (see Panel A7 discussion).

3. SHADOW MARKER PETROGLYPHS

Shadow marker petroglyphs inside the Gap Narrows record specific dates. For every calendar date there are two or more equally precise cairns. The full range of calendar dates are also marked by precise sun-shadow petroglyph markers. This field of research is ongoing. To date I have identified 12 shadow markers. (They are discussed in the Gap Narrows Petroglyph Panel sections A, B, F, and G)

A3	Equinox
A9, A10, F10	Summer solstice
B1	Uncertain
B3	Moon southern standstill
B6a	Winter solstice
B6e	Cross-quarter (sunset Nov. 6 and Feb. 5)
B7	Winter cross-quarter
F11	Summer season, Apr. 29 and Aug. 12
G4	Cave, summer solstice gnomon
G9c	Cave, summer season, Apr. 29 and Aug. 12

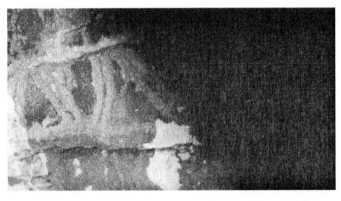

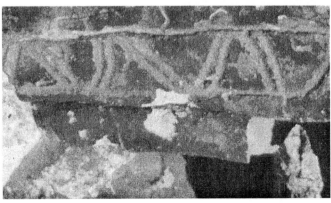

Fig. 3:12—Winter cross-quarter

Sky Watcher's
Sun-Moon-Star Calendar Clock————

From the four corners of the world, to the four corners surrounding the world, to the moss-covered mountains and the oceans, our world is our temple, and when you harm it . . . these are not [just] sacred places, but these are respected and venerated places where the spirits live. And we share this land with the spirits.

> Edmund J. Ladd, Zuni Archaeologist for the National Park Service, Curator of Ethnology at the Museum of New Mexico's Laboratory of Anthropology, Sante Fe (Widdison 1991: 36)

Native American sky watchers from earliest times were recording their observations of the heavens in rocks, art and architecture. Today we call the study of their records "archaeo-astronomy." Sun, moon, and star cycles as the ancients observed and recorded them were their clocks for marking the fixed seasonal life cycles for scheduling agricultural, hunting, gathering, and other annual activities. Ancient homes were built with walls aligned to key horizon sun dates. The calendar was fixed by priests in community temple centers, and could then be duplicated in part on the right dates on household wall calendars with a cross, circle, or lines marking the sunrise shadow movement through a doorway, window or across a post. (I have several wall markers in my own home.)

The Gap calendar served the scheduling needs of the Parowanites well, just as our modern clocks and calendars do today. The variety of ancient clock records is extensive and widespread. Nowhere, not even in the advanced civilization of Mesoamerica, do we see a more developed accurate ancient calendar clock than functioned at the Parowan Gap for over four thousand years.

We should appreciate the origin of our modern clock as an adaptation of nature's clock and not a unique modern invention. A circular reconstruction of the Gap calendar clock illustrates well the universal cosmic composition that dictated our mechanical clock's design. (I am so oriented to the visual harmony of time movement through the four quarters of the day, month, and year reflected in the rotating hands of my watch that I refuse to wear a digital watch.)

I like to think of the Gap calendar clock as an invention that will never fail. It is still ticking away today with the same exact precision as when it was perfected over a thousand years ago. And it will be ticking away a thousand years from now, driven by unfailing solar power. This giant observatory clock is marking the heavenly cycles with nature's precision through the intermeshing time cycles, regardless of whether or not one is at the observatory petroglyphs or cairns to watch it.

Fig. 4:1

This sense of cosmic harmony was so pervasive throughout ancient and modern Native American culture that it is woven into beautiful rugs, clothing designs, works of art, and pottery designs. An ancient, painted Fremont vessel (above) recovered at the Parowan Gap illustrates this concept well. The 45-day cross-quarter may be the best explanation for the 8 sections on the vessel design that splits the 4 quarters into 8 sections (see Fig. 4:2—Clock Wheel, next page). Each has a 3-comb set in a U for the 1.5 moons in a cross-quarter, which is a total of 24 waxing and waning moons for new moon to full moon. The slanting connecting line around the combs gives an impression of rotation that expresses eternal cyclic movement.

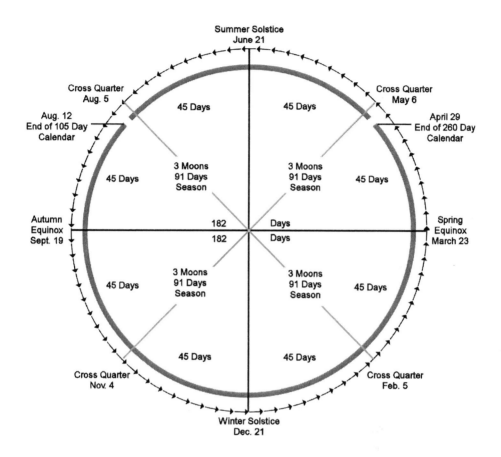

Fig. 4:2—Sun Cycle Day Counts
Fixed cycles, not always fixed dates, were the prime concern
in the ancient Parowan Gap observatory.

SUN

Sighting sticks or rocks can be used to determine the exact solstice standstills by counting days from a mid-equinox when the sun moves its full width each day across the horizon, in contrast to a 5 or 6-day standstill at the solstice north and south ends. Western sunsets are best for tracking the sun to its last gleam precision point. These dominate the Gap observatory. (Sunrise is difficult because the sun bursts suddenly on the eastern horizon then moves up, so it is harder to pinpoint.) Once equinox was determined with equal day counts on each side, the 182 day "half year" points were fixed with Cairn C1 and petroglyph records. The solstices could then be counted as 91 days from equinox. Calendar priests could determine winter solstice with day counts from a fixed horizon feature up to two or three weeks before solstice. This was set up for winter solstice with Cairn H1. Calendar priests also devised an ingenious shadow marker system with parallel lines that essentially worked the same way (see Panels B6 and F10).

The calendar year divided 12 moons to 9, 6 and 3 moon seasons. These were 1.5 moons for 45-day cross-quarters to mark season changes. This divided the year into 8 sections (see Wheel Clock above). There is good evidence for another split into 22–23 days, which is 3 moon quarters. This is pictured on Panel A7 in the 23-comb crescent on the left arm of the V–Gap, which transports 3 moon humanoids with 3 division signs on their bodies for the 3 moon quarters. Two observatory stations (D1, D2) record this 22–23 day cycle after and before the equinoxes on April 15 and August 29. Another 11-day split was documented at Cairn XC1 on April 5, 2005.

The ancient **Sun Calendar** recorded at the Gap is marked by Cairns, Petroglyph counts and Shadow Markers focused on:

Full Year	**364–365 days**
Solstices	(June 21 and Dec. 21)—**182–183 days**
Solstices Equinox	(Sept. 19 and Mar. 23)—**91–92 days** from Solstices
Solstices Equinox Cross-Quarter	(May 6, Aug. 5, Nov. 4, Feb. 5)—**45–46** days which divides the four seasons in half (Lines below the flower are a cross-quarter count)
½ Cross-Quarter	**22–23 days**

Fig. 4:3—Panel B8c

MOON

The erratic **Moon Cycle** observed throughout the Gap area is primarily symbolized by petroglyph "ladders" with circles for moon counts of:

+ 12 (+⅓) moons in a full year
+ 9 moons = human fertility-gestation
+ 6 moon months in a half year (approximately)
+ 3 moon months in a quarter-year season (approximately)

Fig. 4:4

Other moon counts are straight or curving lines marking the divisions of a moon cycle:

+ 7–8 days crescent to quarter (week)
+ 15 days—crescent to full moon (half month)
+ 29–30 days—crescent to quarter to full to quarter to crescent (full month)

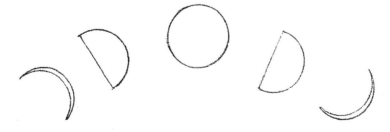

Fig. 4:5

The 19 year Moon Metonic Cycle is recorded on Panel B3a with a 19 section moon ladder in the upper right of the panel adjacent to a natural observation "window" between the cliff wall and a large boulder. On summer solstice, June 21, 2005 we witnessed the Metonic moon rise in the east at dusk right after the sun set in the west. A 5th Century B.C. Greek astronomer named Meton found that the sun and moon have a same day "conjunction" every 19 years. The next Metonic moon rise at summer solstice sunset will be June 21, 2024. (The moon cycles 235 lunations divided by 12 each year = approximately 19 years—moon 235 × 29.5 = 6939 days; sun 365.2 × 19 = 6,939 days).

STARS

The Star Cycle can be observed each night from the south mountain Cave Shelter (Area G) to the top of the opposite north peak where the Polaris North Star "sits." The star constellations rotate in a year around the North Star. Also at night, ancient Sky Watchers observed the Big Dipper move around the North Star. These 7 bright Dipper stars mark the four directions of the heavens—the four seasons of the year. Other star "constellations" were recorded in the Cave Shelter (see Panel G7, page 153). Quoting from *The Mythology of the Americas*, the "Big Dipper or Great Bear is one of the most striking constellations in the northern sky. Because the arrangement of stars is so clear, and it rises and sets in a predictable cycle through the year, it was an important marker of seasonal change among many northern people" (Jones and Malyneaux 2002: 25). The seasonal positions of the Dipper seen at the Gap through the year are, autumn-bottom, winter-east, spring-top, summer-west.

Mesoamerica, Southwest and Great Basin Sacred 260–104 Day Calendar

Mesoamerican scholar Michael Coe has said on numerous occasions that the 260–105 Day Sacred Mayan Calendar was the most important mental construct in Mesoamerican civilization. It is believed to be very ancient, and is thought to have originated as a fixed segment of the agricultural calendar. Discovery of this calendar at Parowan Gap persuades us that ancient migrations occurred between Central America and Utah's Great Basin deserts. Trace analysis of ancient Mexican Aztec turquoise jewelry indicates some turquoise came from mines in Northern Nevada (Harbottle and Weigand, *Scientific American*, 1992: 78–85). Travelers to Northern Nevada from southern regions would have found drainages leading to the Parowan Gap along natural passage routes to their destination northwest into Nevada. The Gap petroglyphs could have been a calendar and compass for ancient land navigators who could also follow hunting "maps" (Panels A10 and C12) and dates of animal and bird migrations to plan hunts for food.

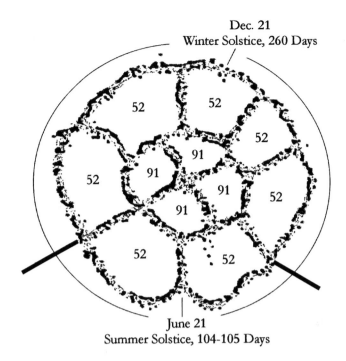

Dec. 21
Winter Solstice, 260 Days

June 21
Summer Solstice, 104-105 Days

Fig. 4:6—Gap Petroglyph Panel C13

Glyph for Sacred 260–104 (105)-day calendar (compare Panel F3, Fig. 11:2, page 126)

7 × 52 days = 364 day year

4 seasons 91 × 4 = 364 day year

The 91 day divisions in the middle are the quarter locations for the Big Dipper at the 4 seasons. Of interest: 7 bright stars define the Big Dipper.

260 day winter animal gestation 5 × 52 = 260

104 day summer planting-harvesting 2 × 52 = 104

"The [Maya] people of Chichicastenango [Highland Guatemala] explicitly offer the period of human gestation as an explanation for the 260-day cycle . . . [which is] nine lunations, each consisting of slightly less than 29 days—or the same number of months a woman is pregnant" (Tedlock, 1982: 93). A moon month, 29 days × 9 months = 261 days. Other mammals have a similar gestation cycle which is ruled by nature. Animals mate in the fall after building body nutrients during the rich summer grazing season and give birth in the spring so newborns can grow through the warm and fertile summer to survive the return of winter. Ancient native cultures had high infant mortality rates, so they learned from the animals to have their babies in the spring with the warm growing season following.

The 260-day Fremont calendar at the Gap is recorded as an integral part of the lunar-solar agricultural year tied to the 9 month human gestation cycle. This Gap record is the first known illustration in the Southwest that the 260-day calendar is a fixed segment of the ancient agricultural year which was between the dates of August 12th and April 29th with winter solstice in the center of the 9 months.

The year is accordingly divided into two life cycle seasons: 105-day summer planting-growing season and 260-day animal winter fertility-gestation season. This idealized division of the yearly life cycle is nature's way of perpetuating life on earth. The spring new born child needs warmth and nutrition from summer, like other animals, to gain sufficient strength to survive the next winter.

Calendar Months
260–105 Day (365 Days) Agricultural Calendar

1. May–**Apr. 29**   Starts 105-day summer planting-growing season May 5 cross-quarter starts 91-day lunar summer quarter

2. June–June 21   Summer solstice; **center of 105-day growing cycle**

3. July   Agriculture, plants mature

4. Aug.–Aug. 5   Autumn cross-quarter harvest time **Aug. 12 starts 260-day winter gestation cycle**

5. Sept.–Sept. 20   Autumn equinox, mid-quarter season

6. Oct.

7. Nov.–Nov. 5   Cross-quarter starts winter quarter season

8. Dec.–Dec. 21   Winter solstice, **center of 260-day gestation cycle**

9. Jan.   Animal fetus matures

10. Feb.–Feb. 5   Cross-quarter starts spring season

11. Mar.–Mar. 21   Spring equinox, mid-quarter season

12. Apr.–**Apr. 29**   **End of 260-day fertility gestation cycle,** Spring birthing season

Astronomer Dr. John Pratt states, "Anciently (around 3000 B.C.), four bright stars marked the four seasons when the sun aligned with them in its annual course through the sky. They were known as the four royal stars, being Aldebaran (spring), Regulus (summer), Antares (fall), and Fomalhaut (winter). I personally have found evidence that the year was also sometimes divided into seven equal parts of 52 days each, and that three additional stars marked those positions, being Procyon (late summer), Spica (late summer), and Altair (late fall). Two of these stars are positioned especially well to do that job: the sun passes Spica 55 days after Regulus, and Altair 53 days after Antares. The center of the great circle of these stars lies in the northern sky. I believe those seven stars are also related to the seven bright stars in the Big Dipper" (Personal communication).

Venus Morning/Evening Star Cycle and Cross-Weave Petroglyphs

Given the level of astronomical knowledge recorded at the Parowan Gap, it should not be surprising to find a record of the Venus Morning/Evening Star observations. Venus petroglyphs are recorded on Panels A7, A10, C5, G2, Area H in the Gap Narrows and Area J by the Little Salt Lake. Venus has an erratic path for its 584-day synodic year. The cross-weave petroglyph most commonly symbolizes the criss-cross movement in the sky that is typical of the Venus star cycle. Detailed discussions of the Venus Star are in the C Area H and Venus-Sun-Moon Conjunctions Sections.

Venus rises in the east just before the sun during its Morning Star phase. Venus goes through three phase shifts before returning as Morning Star. The target numbers in the complete Venus Cycle are based on the Aztec record:

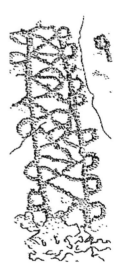

243	Morning Star visibility
+	
77	Invisible days between Morning and Evening Star
+	
252	Evening Star to Morning Star (first appearances)
+	
12	Invisible days return to Morning Star heliacal rise
584	= Total days of the complete Venus Cycle

(Malmstrom 1997: 217)

Fig. 4:7

Bird Cosmic Figures at the Gap

Fig. 4:8—Parowan Gap Bird Petroglyphs

a. Bird man, bird arms and hand

b. Fremont god with bird hand

c. Sun

d. Snow Geese October migration to Sevier Valley (Sevier Lake and Sevier River Map)

e. Eagle form compared on calendar panel

f. Polaris god with bird hand

g. Eagle or condor entering cave with sun

h. Eagle (?) with prey

i. Bat

j. Owl on Lunar panel

k. Flying serpent (bird legs)

l. Humanoid with bird wings

m. Condor

n. Man-bird feet and hands with comet

o. Humanoid with bird hands and arm-wings

p. Humanoid with bird wing-arms

q. Caracara (Birds soar high like eagles)

r. Caracara bird

Interpretive Tour Guide — Through the Gap Narrows

The tour is organized counter-clockwise in eight areas,
labeled A–H (see map next page, Fig. 5)

Note: Petroglyph Panels are numbered from the original Gap
Project reports archives. Missing numbers belong to excluded,
more obscure panels.

Petroglyph Panels Location Map

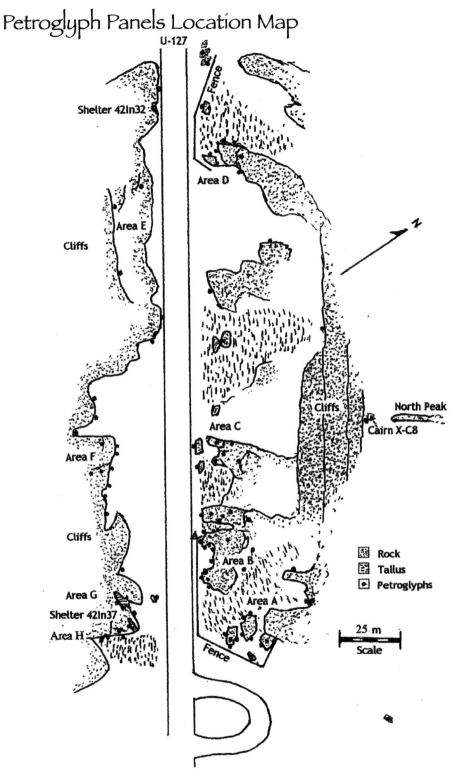

Fig. 5—Gap Narrows Area Map

Area A

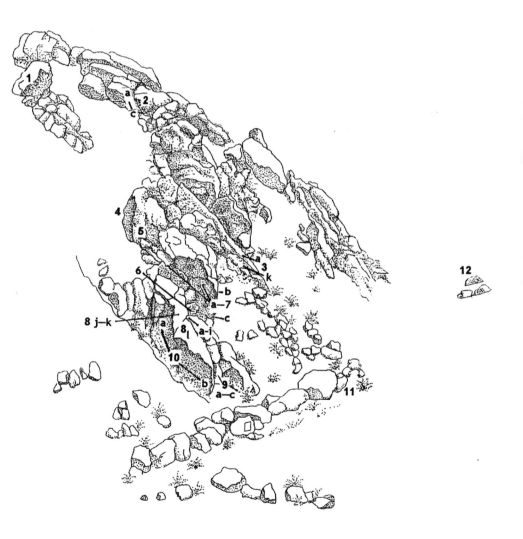

Fig. 6—Area A Cliffs Map
Area A is on the east end of the Narrows, north side, facing east.

Panel A1

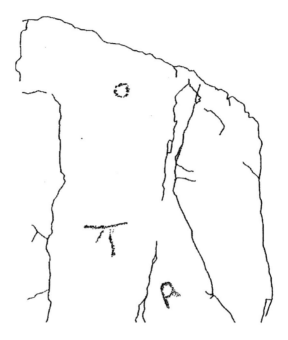

Fig. 6:1

High on a large remote rock overlook eastward is a simple panel with only two circles and three lines. This might be where the ancient sky watchers began observing the heavens and pecking their sky charts in the rocks.

With this introduction, we are left to ponder sun and moon shifting movements through the year's eternal life cycles, which is an ongoing discovery in the hundreds of petroglyphs recorded at the Gap.

This high simple panel introduces the four basic paths of the sun, moon, and stars in the heavens. A sun circle at the top is above a vertical rise path line. A short slanted line was later scratched to the side to show the actual angle of rise. The horizontal path line is the north-south movement along the horizon. A moon circle to the lower right pictures the moon after rising in the east on its setting descent angle path in the west. The moon also has a west-to-east progression from new moon to full moon and back to new moon through its monthly cycle (see Panel A2).

Panel A2

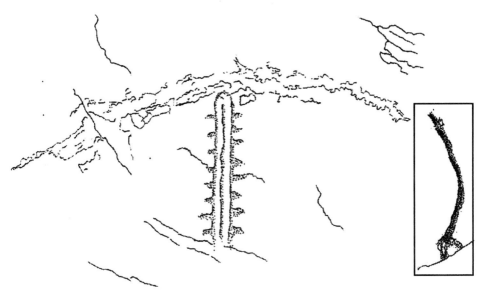

Fig. 6:2

This lunar panel has a natural reddish arch in the rock at the top that was adopted to picture the moon's path across the sky through the month. The petroglyph under the arch rises on a vertical path line to full moon through two quarters symbolized by the 8-comb count on both sides of the glyph. This is the basic form of "umbrella trees" pictured on several other panels.

A 40 cm.-wide table rock at the bottom of the panel has a deeply grooved channel pecked to the edge (see inset) that could collect rain water for ritual use. It might also have been used to collect blood from animal sacrifice.

Panel A3

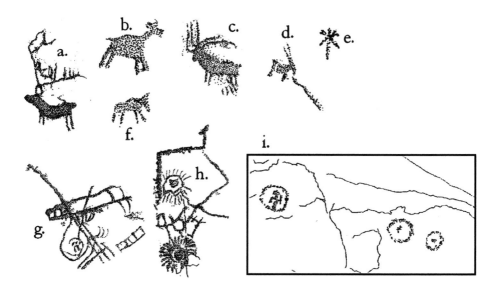

Fig. 6:3

a. Elk shedding velvet from antlers (occurs August–September each year)

b. Goat

c. Elk

d. Spike Elk

e. Lizard

f. Moose Cow

g. V–Gap Map

h. Serpent over sun trails

i. Equinox sun watcher in sunrise circle spotlight

This large black panel slopes along the north fence line of Area A. It is damaged and difficult to see. This is the only panel at the Gap with a variety of big game animals (compiled in the figure above). The V–Gap map on this panel gives the impression that the Narrows pass was used at times for big game hunting drives (see Panels A7 and A8). The most outstanding feature is the equinox sun watcher on the south vertical face of this panel (lower right). The sunwatcher sights across his raised hand east to two concentric suns (equinoxes). A prominent dot on his circle sight line forms the first point of light on this surface at the first equinox sunrise.

Panel A4

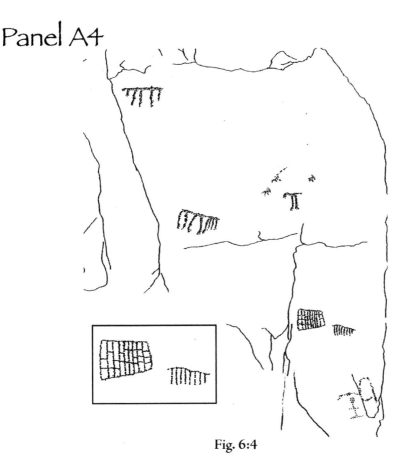

Fig. 6:4

On a hunch, I sized and overlaid the spiral on the terrain map (Fig. 3:10 bottom), and found each distinctive turn of the spiral matches closely with the observatory cairns between summer solstice and equinox. Fantastic as it may seem, this could map that system.

Panel A4 is located above the main Panel A7 where the viewer looks east. I believe this panel is a basic introduction to the Parowan Gap calendar system. Its rock face has:

- Top 5-comb = 5 lines for 4 cross-quarter divisions (equinox to equinox)—2 shorter side divisions match shorter equinox days; 2 longer center divisions match longer summer days.

- Middle right bird (Caracara) stands by 3 small (distant?) big horn sheep to possibly signify the migratory season.

- Bottom right checker board "box" has 30 sections for 1 month.

- Adjacent 8-comb (by "box") equals a lunar quarter (week) or 8 cross-quarters in a year.

- Below is a half circle sign for a quarter-moone by a sky watcher.

- Similar 8-comb (middle-left) is in front of the bird.

This panel, also hidden high in the rocks is basic astronomy following Panel A1. It is a simple time cycles account for the year recorded in a numbers code box and three combs. In the bottom right corner, a sky watcher stick figure introduces the panel with his body lines conforming to adjacent sun-moon horizontal and vertical movement lines. He could be a god image controlling the movement, which is recorded overhead, first in a 7-day comb expanding left from new moon to first quarter. A moon box has the full moon record in 30-day spaces for the month. It is designed with a variety of spatial combinations which could additionally be read as moon and sun cycle counts (see Sky Watcher section).

Moon counts are everywhere at the Gap because the moon gives the most visual day tracking through 4-quarter weeks in the month and 3-moon seasons. We will refer to them constantly on our trek through the Gap. The moon is one fascinating heavenly body that gives us so many gifts, both physically and philosophically, as we shall see.

Large migratory water fowl typically have morning and evening flight circuits between lakes and feeding grounds. Some flocks may have flown west from the Little Salt Lake to feeding grounds. Bird hunts would have involved pre-arranged snares and blinds built in feeding grounds and around water shorelines. Martin Tyner of Southwest Wildlife Reserve has assisted with information on bird habitats and flight patterns.

Panel A7a

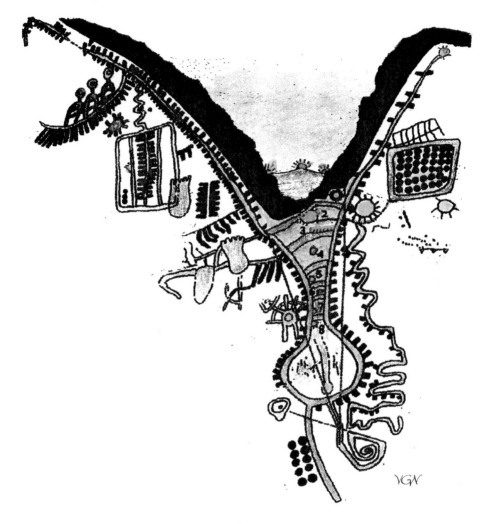

Fig. 6:5—Time and Terrain
Calendar V–Gap Map

The impressive V–Gap Calendar glyph is the first large glyph that Gap visitors see when they park by the fence in Area A at the east end of the Gap Narrows. Some say "This is Indian graffiti"! Animals and a few hunting scenes are obvious, but a lot of imaginative "rock art" was considered ancient Indian "child's play" with animals, circles, dots and unrealistic stick figures. The brass plaque installed in the fence in 1960 reflects the belief that most Indian petroglyphs cannot be interpreted. Until our full scale archaeological investigation found interpretive keys, this view prevailed for over half a century in Utah Fremont archaeology.

The V shape figure pictures the Gap Narrows from its eastern approach (see terrain overlay figure). The panel has over 80 figures. Precision drawings by Lance Harding, with my assistance, have helped to facilitate the calendar study. The tics around the large "V" (including attached counting combs) record the sun's 182-day (half year) horizon sunsets between winter and summer solstice. This includes some specifically dated events. In the middle of the "V" picture, the sun circles that are by horizon lines picture sunsets that are viewed from observation cairns in the east basin for solstices (182 days), equinoxes (91 days) and intermediate cross-quarters (45 days). The bottom circle of the petroglyph represents the east basin (see Astronomy Record Section). The line off the bottom of it represents observatory trails from the cairns. Two rows of 5 dots on the side of this "trail" represent the 5 observatory cairns for the half year sun transit, repeated for the second half. (see Astronomy "Wheel Clock" section for a thorough discussion.)

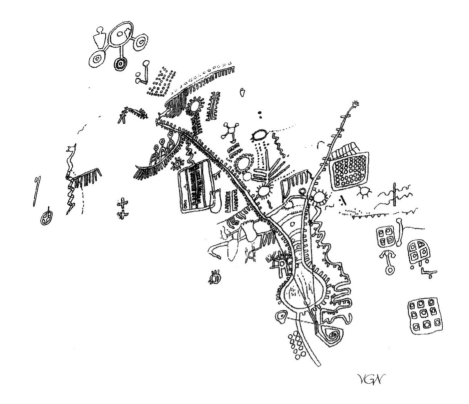

YGN

Fig. 6:6—V–Gap Calendar Petroglyph

Proof of 41 tics on the right arm is in the attached box with 41 dots that highlight this important date. The prospect of a New Year anchor date that could lay out the whole calendar record here with the observatory inspired an exhaustive study of this panel. The following summarizes results for decoded New Year plus solstice, equinox, and 260-day calendar cycle day counts. Left arm tics—125, right arm tics—40 or 41, 3 attached combs 6 + 7 + 4 = 17 totaling 182 or 183—a half year.

6-comb above summer solstice (middle) setting sun

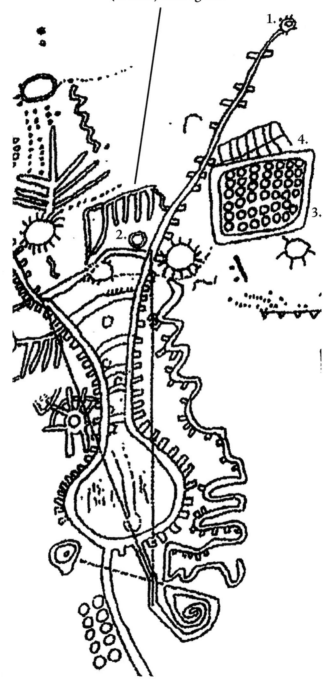

Fig. 6:7—(right arm)

1. Half year day-count can only be accurately made from equinox (Sept. 20/Mar. 21), counting days to the solstices and back to locate the mid-point. So the equinox test starts at the top right arm sun.

2. Key to the right arm top date is in the observatory map correlation between the arms. The top horizon sunset (concentric circle) in the Narrows map (as viewed from the spiral observatory Cairn B2) records April 29–30 (left) and May 5 cross-quarter (right) with the 6-comb above the setting sun marking the day span difference.

3. The odd dot in the lower right corner of the big box, and odd tic at the bottom of the lobe circle are for date adjustments (odd days and leap year shifts).

4. The 40–41 dots in the upper box and right arm tics count the days from equinox (March 20) to April 29–30.

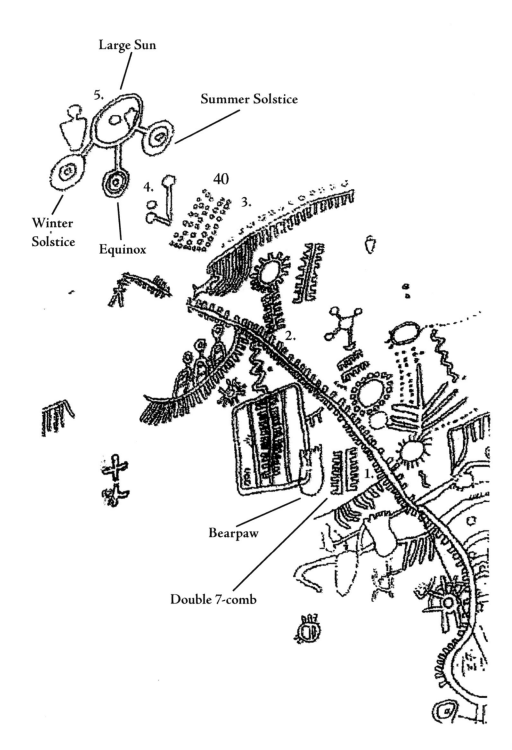

Fig. 6:8—(left arm)

1. Confirmation may be found in another 52-day count following April 29–30. There are, in fact, 52 days up the left arm from the bottom break up to the summer solstice sun growing the corn plant by the adjacent 7-comb, (including the three comb counts to that point: 35 + 7 + 4 + 6 = 52).

2. Another 52 count up the left arm, to complete the 105-day summer season on August 12, reaches the contact point with a double 7-comb for full moon with a 15-ray full moon on top which is inset into a comb recess above, with 15 teeth. This full comb is a half cross-quarter that actually records the 260-day cycle. A bear inset into the left side of the comb signifies starting the autumn fertility gestation cycle. The other 20 teeth in front of the bear multiplied by 13 dots across the comb's top (reconstructed from Utah State History archive photo) would be 260, implying a link with the Mesoamerican 260-day sacred calendar. The final clincher for the 260-day cycle is to locate its full day count. An additional 78 count added to the 182 half year on the V–Gap map is needed. What is in the two large combs and moon box? 23 + 23 + 30 = 76—just two short. And now the little 2-comb attached to the moon box's side adds 2 and claims the crown for the 260-day cycle. Total 78 + 182 = 260!

3. The figures at the top, rising above the long comb add further confirmation. A cluster of 40 dots, matching the right arm's 40–41 box, rises up in alignment with the 20th tooth in the comb's left side. The obvious mirrored day-count is from August 12 to autumn equinox at the left arm's tip to complete the half year.

4. Two circle arms above the 40-box point to the big 4-circle sun glyph at the top for the year's solstices and equinox. The sun arms below focus on the center equinox and right summer solstice suns. Notice the floating circle next to the left "equinox" arm. This is the relative position of August 12 to equinox, not cross-quarter as initially thought.

5. The large concentric sun at the top has three hanging suns, each with 3-concentric circles for the 3-moon quarters center on equinox (middle), winter solstice (left), and summer solstice (right). This is a very basic perception of the sun's 6-month solar transit across the horizon, swinging back and forth eternally between its solstice standstills like a clock pendulum. The origin and control of this heavenly phenomenon runs deeper. The Fremont god on top of the left winter solstice governs the sun's cyclical shifts. A

small Fremont god inside the top circle is really the governing cosmic navel, where the god dwells at the center of the universe and all things move round about him. This is none other than the Polaris governing center depicted in detail on the cave shelter Panel G7 with the Polaris Fremont god in control.

There are a great many more details recorded on this V–Gap panel that could be introduced, but that would require another book. Various references will be made to this panel in other Sections and Panel discussions.

Zoomorphs outside the calendar counts of the panel include: big horn sheep at the bottom, 3 bear paws above, and 2 mammals by a raised serpent at left center.

The Venus glyphs at the lower right of the V–Gap map are discussed with Area H and J Panels.

Panel A7b

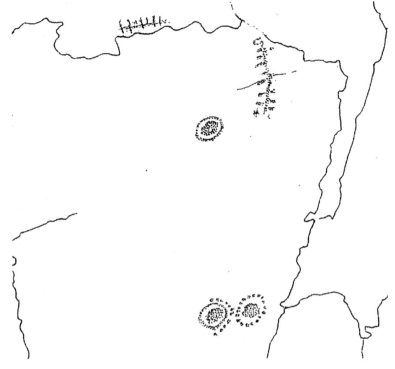

Fig. 6:9

At the top of this panel (A7b) the figures are around the right edge from A7a. Isolated high on the panel, A7b has:

+ Three concentric circles—2 together have 11 and 19 dots = 30-day moon cycle (also may code the 19 year lunar metonic cycle).

+ 2 weathered double combs above record possible lunar day counts.

Panel A7c

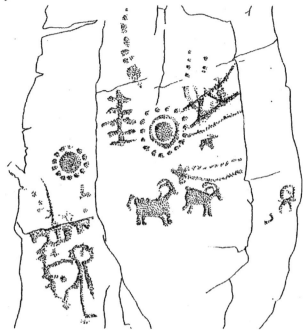

Fig. 6:10

A7c, below A7b, has the following calendar glyphs:

+ Middle concentric circle with 16 dots = full moon below rows of weathered dots.

+ Another circle (left) with 13 dots = 13 moon cycles in a lunar/solar year (12 full and 1 partial).

+ Double comb in the middle with 5 teeth on each side suggests the 5 prime cairns for each half of the solar transit between solstices. (Compare 2 rows of 5 dots by the map "observatory trail" at the base of the V–lobe on panel A7a.)

+ Man (with outstretched arms) stands on a trail above two big horned sheep with small sheep above and at right, for an apparent hunting drive. Nine upper trail dots could be a hunting tally.

+ This panel section may be a ritual calendar association with big horn sheep fertility and hunting. As I interpret it, a Fremont god has outstretched arms along a row of nine dots for a nine month fertility-gestation cycle along a parallel trail line that contacts a mother sheep below with a father sheep behind, and two kids.

+ Lower left panel has recent pecking with a human's stick figure that appears to be modern graffiti.

Panels A8J–A9B

Panel A8j

To the left of the V–Gap Panel is another large flat faced rock that has four panel sections. Many of the petroglyphs are damaged from weathering. The visible figures on the upper sections are most interesting. At the top left a trail map extends from a place dot into the distance around 9 bends next to footprints by another place dot signifying a destination. Based on its orientation, this could be a trail map from a location in the east end of the Parowan Gap pass. At the right, a 20 cm.-wide 3-concentric sun has 20 dots in its outer ring for 20 days, possibly in the 3rd month of a quarter (80 days).

Panel A8k—Falling Comet

The central figure is a falling comet. Three rows of 28 dots at the upper left side of its four light streamers could record the event. A radiant sun circle at the upper right with 10 rays and a 4-comb could also date the event. This may well be a record of Halley's comet that appears every 74 years and is a majestic spectacle for a few months, which last appeared in 1986. It would have been recorded here in A.D. 846, 992, 998, or 1074. A humanoid with exaggerated bird talon hands and feet signifying "flight" of this spirit being points to the comet. On his left, a series of weathered dots extend up from his hand in an arch by a sky serpent to a circle high up. This personage appears to be a spirit companion of the comet. Comets were traditionally thought to be omens of ill fortune.

Panel A8l—Big Horned Sheep

The slopping damaged panel below has an unusually large, 30 cm.-long big horn sheep facing a split trail, which could be the Narrows pass on the left as pictured. It could be a sheep drive into the Narrows trap. A 5th longer leg at the rear with a cloven foot may be a sign for multiple sheep involved in a drive.

Panel A9a

In a recess at the base of the cliff below Panel A8 is a petroglyph with meandering lines and two large circles (spiral and concentric circle). On a summer morning I observed the shadow line bisect the two circles along the straight base line.

Panel A9b—Protective Serpent

A raised serpent over two sun disks represents the path of the rising sun. Twelve long lines and one short line count the 12 and a third moons in a solar year. The circle beneath with 7 lines may be the 7th month of the year. The figures were composed to the sun shadow that silhouettes the left side.

Fig. 6:11—(center) Effigy Topography Maps

Panel A10

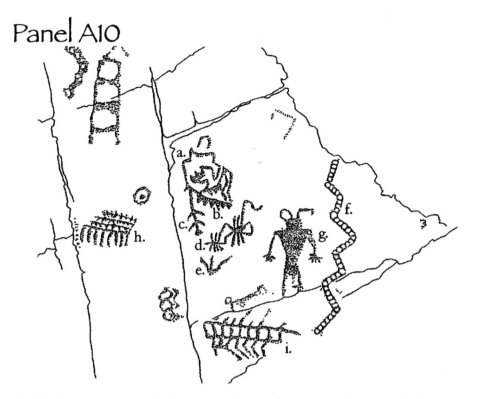

At the Gap in 1995, I asked Alva Matheson about the spider petroglyph on Panel A10. He related that the Spider Woman in Paiute tradition resided on a mountain top and that her legs were viewed as the ridges coming off the mountain peak. Curiously, I had previously deciphered this spider petroglyph as a map of the south peak of the Red Hills with the six legs matching the slope ridges most visible with melting winter snow.

Trail Maps:

a. Red Hills north hunting trails

b. Gap south pass hills

c. Lizard maps-basin south pass and ridges

d. 2 spiders maps – south Red Hills ridges

e. Bird track maps – Red Hills south pass

f. Sun serpent 45 dots = 45 days from May 5–August 5 cross-quarters counts to solstice

g. Spider woman antennae like left spider antennae

h. Lunar quarter combs count

i. 29-day lunar "weaving" count

Fig. 6:12
Petroglyph matching features to topographic map (Fig. 6:13).

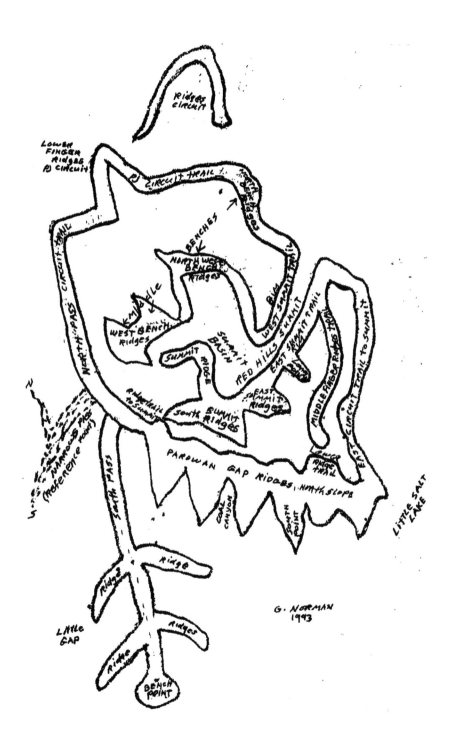

Fig. 6:13 (Norman 2002)

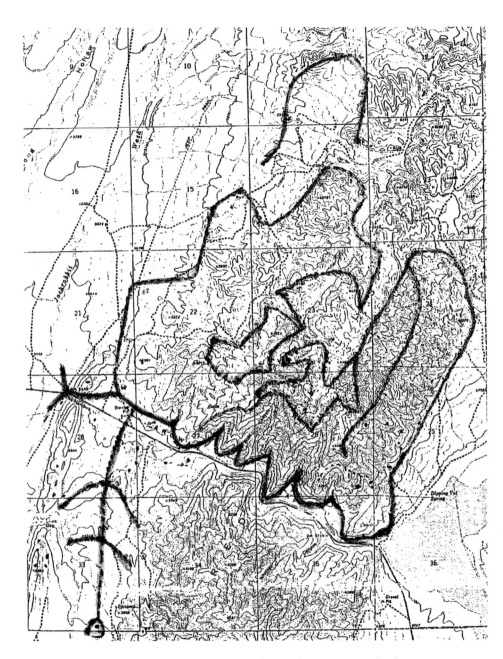

Topographic map correlates with Panel A10a petroglyph map.

Panel A10a

Summer Fertility Serpent

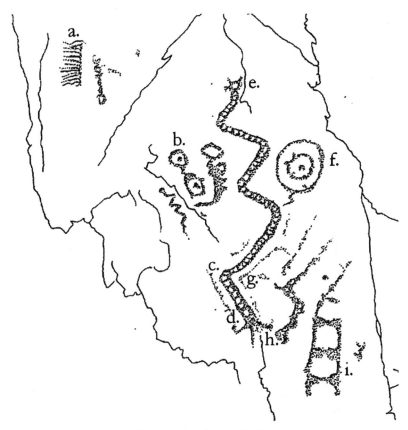

Fig. 6:14—(upper left)

a. 12.5 month comb for lunar year

b. Venus serpent (see Panel J1c discussion)

c. May 5–6

d. April 29

e. 52 dots = day count to summer Solstice from April 29–30

f. Summer Solstice Sun

g. 45-day cross-quarter (top 5 sections)

h. Bird legs

i. Ladder = 3 moons

The Venus Horned-Serpent-Bird figure with 52 dots in its undulating body related to the 260–105-day sacred calendar. There is a 52-day count from April 29 to summer solstice followed by 52 days again to August 12 for the 105-day summer growing season. At summer solstice before sunset in 2005 when this panel is in shadow, I somewhat by chance discovered the large concentric sun section is illuminated by the setting sun with the shadow line along the serpent body, which confirmed my discovery (see page 174 for detailed analysis).

Panel A10b
Fremont Spider Woman Weaving "Time"

Spider web "antennae" on the head of this spider woman ties to the spider woman on A10 center panel. Based on the Paiute tradition of the spider woman, her bird hands and feet signify flight with the sun and moon. Her right antennae is oriented to and in the shape of the weaving design above it. Various Indian traditions relate the spider woman weaving time with the moon in the night sky. (The sun is a father-male symbol. The moon is a mother-female symbol.)

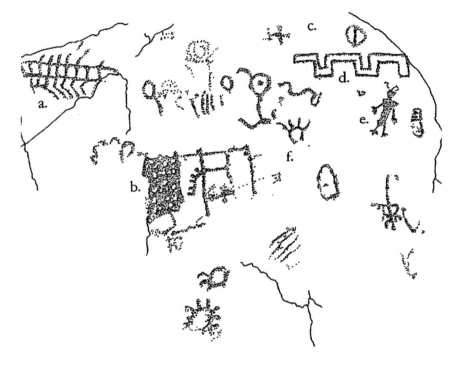

Fig. 6:15—(right)

    a. 29-day lunar weaving count

    b. Lunar-solar box

    c. Split moon rise, moon watcher

    d. Squared weaving pattern

    e. Spider woman with bird hands and feet

    f. Numerous suns and pathlines

Area B

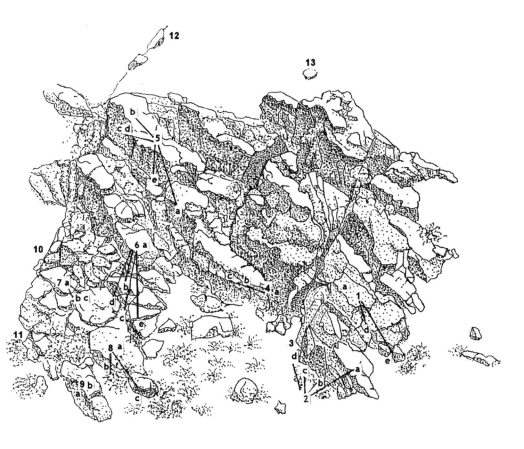

Fig. 7—Area B Cliffs Map
Area B extends on the road into the Gap Narrows
beyond a large talus quarry slide.

Panel B2b

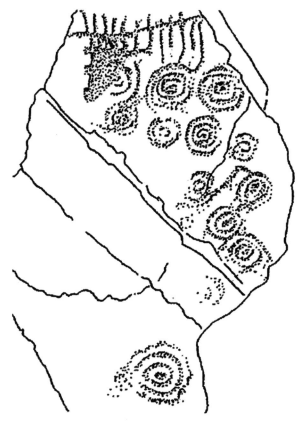

Fig. 7:1

A unique large boulder in front of a cliff face is covered with 13 concentric sun circles. There are 13 moons in a solar year (12 full moons and 1 short moon cycle completes 365 days). A dot with 3 concentric circles depicts a 3-month quarter. A bear paw at the top overlaps a 3-concentric circle, and its five claws connect to a double 22-comb (half cross-quarter). Two notches on the paws side may double the count. This boulder could be a simple introduction to the Gap calendar observatory at the east entrance to the Narrows.

Panel B1a
Sky Watcher's Calendar Observations Record

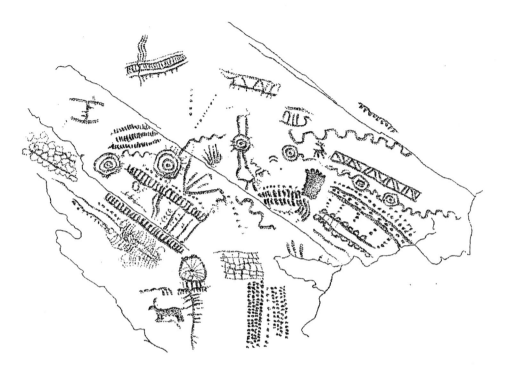

Fig. 7:2

This large, involved panel contains some of the most carefully pecked figures at the Gap. Calendar counts include dots, circles, lines, ladders, boxes, combs and wavy lines to record sun and moon cycles. The wavy line at the top right has "13 turns" (a year). A big horned sheep beside this line faces a 9 triangle panel (9 moons gestation time). The next wavy line below the triangle glyph has 3-concentric sun circles attached for the three main seasons (summer-left, autumn-center, winter-right). The extensive calendar records on this impressive panel were doubtless made by different sky watchers over many years.

Panel B1b
Sky Watcher's Calendar Glyph

Fig. 7:3—(lower right of Panel B)

Below Panel B is another 12 turn (year) vertical wavy line in deeply grooved bas relief. Four dots at its side record the four seasons. The 5-comb at the left may refer to the 5 primary sun transit observation cairns in the east basin for the year (see Cairn Map). The large concentric sun (bottom middle) rises over the head of a sky watcher with raised hands. This is a vivid figure for a sun watcher related to the record on this panel. A bird track (flight) above points up to a line of 5 dots off a sheep's leg in a row of 5 big horn sheep which may symbolize the journey of the sun through the 5 solar transit observatory stations.

Panel B3a
Owl / Moon Share Night Sky

This panel was first analyzed as a lunar Metonic record by Nal Morris for the Parowan Gap project (1995, 1998). This discussion reflects in part some of his observations. Further study with a detailed accurate drawing by Lance Harding revealed additional insights.

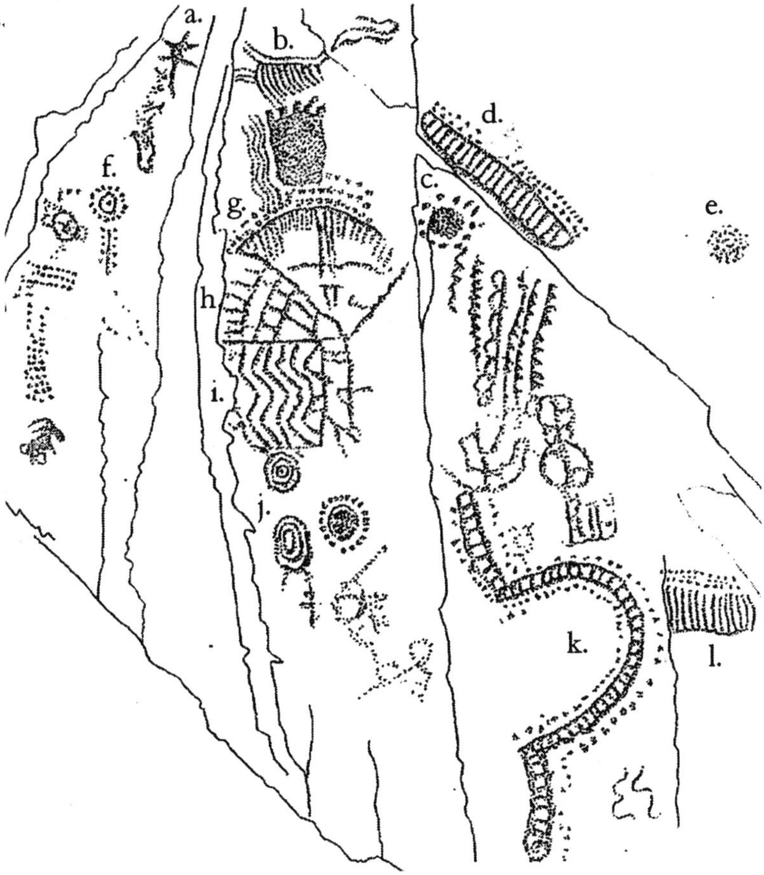

Fig. 7:4

a. Lizard
b. Owl
c. 12 moons year circle
d. 19-year Metonic Cycle
e. Moon shadow marker (inside rock cleft illuminated by moonrise June 21, 2005)
f. 15-day full moon count circle.
g. Lunation "Fan" with 29 lines; middle line marks full moon
h. Wedge records four 3-month quarters and 6 months
i. 5.5 wavy lines with 16 turns = full moon
j. Two 3-month quarter circles, 15 dots count full-moon time
k. Crescent moon serpent 52 segments; total day count dots on sides unclear
l. Thirteen comb + rows of 30 dots = 13 moon-months in the year

The nocturnal owl, symbol for the moon, is perched over a lunation count. One evening while I was discussing this panel with two tourists, a full moon rose on the eastern horizon. As it came into full view an owl flew from its cliff nest above and perched on a rock pinnacle at the east end of the Narrows and gazed at the moon. This transported me back in time 1,000 years when a sky watcher may have observed the same event that inspired his owl symbol in this petroglyph. The owl petroglyph was first pointed out to me by Martin Tyner, a master falconer, who recognized it as a horned owl. A closer look at the owl confirms this connection. Why is the owl image composed of a bear paw for its body? The owl is a symbol of the night and the bear hibernates through the winter season symbol of the "night" time of the year. The owl's head is shaped from an 11-comb + 1 line overhead totaling a year count. Add 3 lines on the owl's beak to total 15 for a full moon count, which may also symbolize the three moon month seasons. Four wavy lines to the left of the body suggest flying motion of the wings through four seasons.

The fan below the owl has 29-day lines. The fan is an actual picture of the moon's traverse across the sky from new moon in the west to full moon overhead, to last crescent moon in the east. The section below the fan has a 6-comb (6 months) and 4-ladder (4 seasons) and 3-space (3 month quarter).

A large U-shaped (pregnant) serpent at the lower right has 52 count body sections on its body which relates to the 260-day fertility gestation cycle (9 lunar months—see Sky Watcher's section).

The U-shape may symbolize the moon crescent and also a pregnant mother (the moon is a female symbol).

The circle at the top right is inside a cleft formed by the B2 boulder. When I first discovered this circle in 2001, I speculated that it could interact with the moon rise at the lunar southern standstill. On summer solstice, June 21, 2005, the moon rose at its southern extreme standstill and indeed illuminated this circle with a shadow line around its left side and bottom. My respect grew for the ancient sky watchers from observing this event. This occurs once every 18.6 years in the moon's Metonic cycle. The upper right 19-step ladder (nearest whole number to 18.6) records this cycle and points toward the circle behind the boulder. A 5th century B.C. Greek astronomer named Meton found that the sun and moon have a same day "conjunction" every 19 years. The moon cycle's 235 lunations divided by 12 each year = approximately 19 years. (moon 235 × 29.5 = 6939 days or 19 years; sun 365.2 × 19 = 6939 days or 19 years).

Panel B4a

Panel B4a has calendar counts for sun and moon cycles. Count the numbering glyphs and decide which calendar events are recorded. Animals are near migration-trail lines.

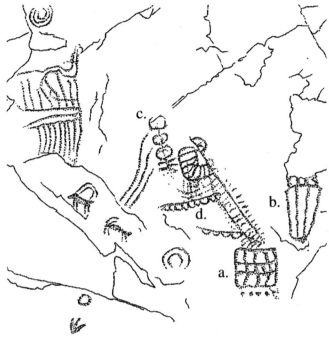

Fig. 7:5

a. Lower right box has 13 segments = 13 new moons in a year.

b. Long box above pictures 3-month quarter (1 season) 3 moons on top.

c. Center line with 3 circles = same as (b).

d. Below is a line with 9 circles and to the left is a 9-comb, both suggesting the 9 months gestation cycle.

Panel B6a
Winter Solstice Day-Plot Shadow Marker

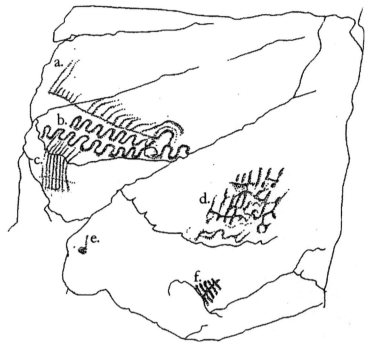

Fig. 7:6

a. Comb; 15+ day teeth before winter solstice turn around loop at right end
b. Two wavy lines = Month counts
c. Eight hanging lines = Day shadow markers preceding winter solstice
d. Combs maze; weathered
e. Sun circle with sunrise path line
f. Tree with 5 branches on both sides

I first observed winter solstice sunrise shadow cast on this panel in 1995. Later Joel Clements assisted with observations to decipher day progressions in the close parallel lines leading to the winter solstice mark. Hopi Calendar Priest's project the winter solstice date in a similar way for scheduling their winter solstice-new year festival events. The results of our study determined that observations could be started about 3 weeks before solstice (December 1–21). A visible sunrise during that period could pinpoint solstice. A sun circle with a line at the lower right is silhouetted at the solstice.

Fig. 7:7
Day progression shadow line markers to winter solstice

Panel B6e
Winter Season Shadow Marker

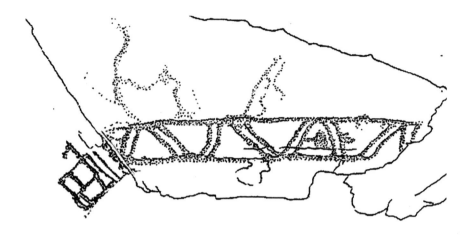

Fig. 7:8—Triangle bands panel

The triangle panel has 8 angle lines. A circle with a line inside one triangle is a sign for the sun shadow (see Panel B6a). The left end of this panel wraps around the edge of the ledge with 5 dots that tie to a segmented box with 5 sections. Measuring this box and the triangle panel reveals increments of a possible standard measure which would explain the unusual extension on the panel. The photo shows the winter cross-quarter sunset shadow on the middle triangle (November 5 and February 5). Other shadow dates may be recorded on the other triangles.

Fig. 7:9—Winter cross-quarter

Panel B7a
Spider Web Winter Season Shadow Marker

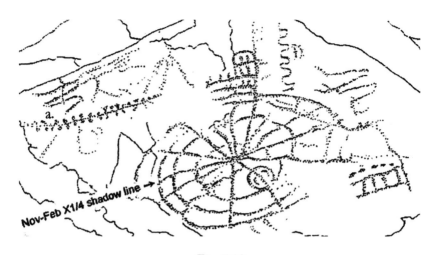

Fig. 7:10
Line with 30 tics over a U-moon sign = moon-month count

This panel is located high up on an upward slanting table rock at the west end of Area B cove. A large (50 cm.) spider web is surrounded by weathered remains of typical line and dot counts. It has 13 full length spokes through the spiral's 3 ½ turns. A small concentric circle attached to the right (north) spoke labels the spider web's lunar-solar function. To the right, a ladder with 4 steps (4 full moons) has 5 dots above it (5 observatory stations?). A November and February winter cross-quarter sunrise shadow line (cast by the cliff face of Panel B1) bisects the circle. The web's 3 ½ spiral circles begin and end on this shadow line. Divisions of the spider web may be calendar counts but are uncertain due to weathering.

A line at the upper left has 30 tics for the month day-count. Other lines and dots at the top are weathered.

Panel B8a
V~Lobe Gap Calendar Map

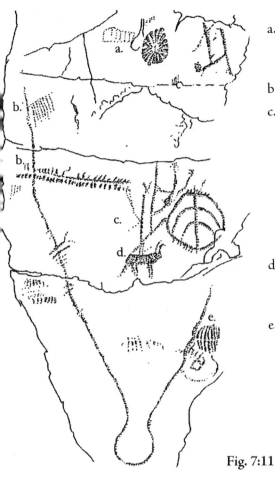

a. Six section moon-ladder by a deep-grooved 15–16 grooved "full" moon symbol

b. Weathered calendar count

c. Large moon "shield" by V right arm. Seven day-tics on the top and bottom plus two crescents on the inside picture moon quarter phases to full moon apex vertical line (Position by V right arm relates to Panel A7 and marks the 105-day summer season)

d. Path line from moon to animal may relate to the fall mating and winter gestation seasons

e. A ball of vertical lines split across the middle totals 15 for another "full" moon count

Fig. 7:11

This large (8 ft.) panel is on a slanting rock inside the B Group cove. A large V–lobe surrounding the panel duplicates the V–lobe on Panel A7 as a map for the Narrows. A few tic marks are on the left arm like the Panel A7 V–Gap map. The main counts, however, are adjacent and inside the V of this panel. A row of 30 lines crosses the left arm above for a lunation. Eight other lines by the arm above equals a lunar quarter. At the top center is a deeply grooved circle with 17 or 18 spokes. The main figure in the center is a sun shield with two crescents inside bisected by a vertical line. The six sections may be the two 3-month seasons for a half year. The path line comes off the shield to an animal on a trail line below.

Panel B8c
Turning of Winter Season
on Cross-Quarter Axis

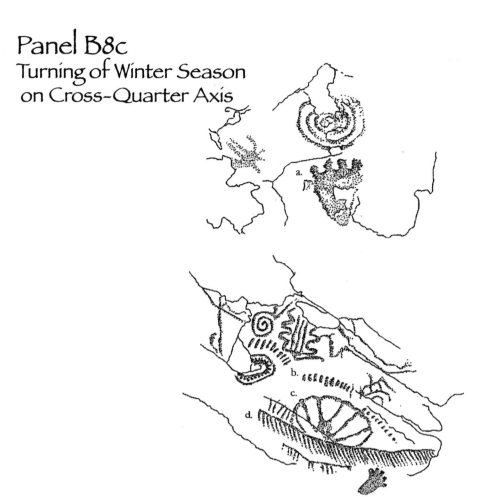

Fig. 7:12

a. A bear paw with 4 toes counts a 4-month spiral above through winter hibernation (November through February).

b. Below, two lines with 10 tics and one with 9 tics total 29 days for a month count.

c. The rock side has a 6-segment sun "flower" with a 6-comb attached for a half year projected on a path line left to summer solstice.

d. A 46-comb line with a footprint below for a cross-quarter slopes upward to the left in line with the 6-month comb.

The reverse may also be applicable with a cross-quarter descent to winter solstice. From this location a sightline to winter cross-quarter sunrise (November 5) is visible to the east, and the reverse sightline to summer cross-quarter sunset (May 5) is also visible to the west. This interpretation is very important to the central primary axis of the Parowan Gap deciphered in the hill top cairns (see Parowan Gap Sacred Space Section).

Panel B10a
Trees, Dots, Lattice, and Comb Counts

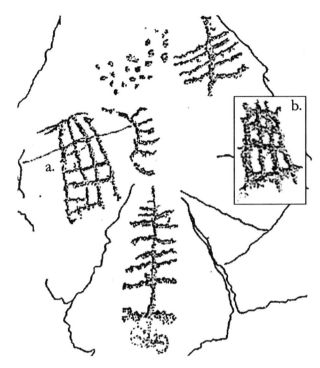

Fig. 7:13

- Bottom Tree Eight   Branches on each side tapers at the top like a juniper; the numbers match moon quarters for a full moon count with two moon circles at the bottom; here a natural counting device in tree branches expresses plant growth with the moon and seasons

- Top Tree   Nine branches grow through the 9-month winter gestation cycle

- Lattice Inset (b.)   Inset from above has three 3-month quarters for 9 months; 4 teeth sign on top for 4 quarters

- Left Lattice (a.)   Thirteen sections equal 13 new moons in a year (one open for 13th part moon)

- 6-Comb   Six-month solar transit with dots above

- Dots   Nineteen dots(?) could record the 19-year lunar Metonic cycle

Panel B11a
Year Cocoon and Spanish Cross

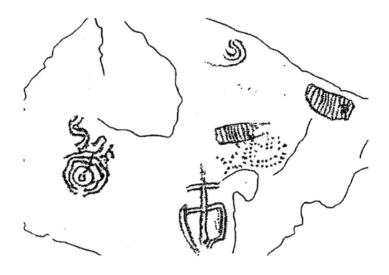

Fig. 7:14

- **Left Serpent Circle**   A "sun" serpent rises on a path from the middle of a three month concentric sun circle.

- **Right Oval Ladder**   A cocoon shaped ladder has 12 steps with a moon circle for the months of a solar year.

- **Center Ladder**   This moon ladder is weathered on the right end and has 45–50 dots below for a possible cross-quarter count.

- **Cross**   A cross with two bars is the Papal Cross; two ribbon streamers on the sides match the crosses that were carried by Spanish explorers; Spanish presence at the Gap is also documented by a brim on a profile head recorded with Gap petroglyphs by the Parley P. Pratt expedition in 1850.

Area C

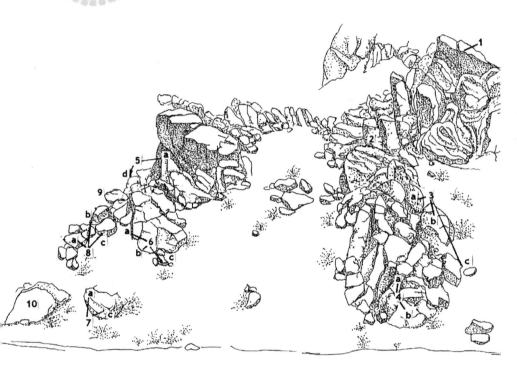

Fig. 8—Area C1–C10 Panels Map
Area C is in the rock outcrops on the north talus
slope in the center of the Narrows.

Panel C3a
Triangles, dots, and wavy line counts

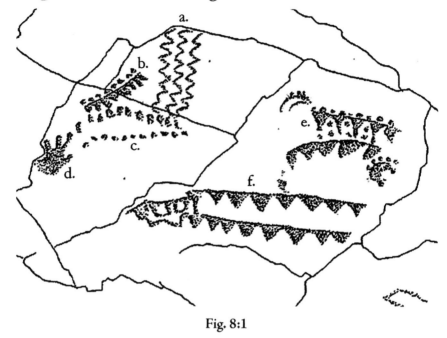

Fig. 8:1

Panel C3 is visible high in the rocks west of the first narrow slide area

a. Three wavy lines with 13 turns each = 3 years

b. Eight-comb with 16 dots = full moon

c. Two rows with 22 dots = half cross-quarter

d. Hand points up to calendar counts

e. Five Fremont god figures in a row with dot counts in between over the top of 5-triangle comb next to a dotted damaged circle

f. Two 8-tooth triangle combs with ½ circles wrapped at left record moon quarters

Other figures below include a diving stick man (not pictured) and a 3-concentric sun circle.

Panel C4

This panel in two sections is next to the road below Panel C3. The upper figure is a cocoon shape of 12 irregular circles with triangular teeth above. This double comb has 11 + 12 teeth for a 23 day half cross-quarter. It could also record 2 years.

Fig. 8:2

The lower panel section has two vertical rows of 6 dots for the two halves of the year. Five dots across the bottom may relate to the sun transit. There are 2 dots at the right below a faint U-moon. The spruce tree at the bottom has 8 branches on both sides for the 2 quarters of a 16-day full moon count. (Compare Panel B10.) These tree figures are found in only two areas—here in the center of the Gap and inside the little cave shelter which suggests a relationship to the tree of life as a cosmic symbol connecting the underworld (roots), earth and the heavens (branches). In Hopi tradition "the arms or branches of the spruce are upraised because the spruce is holy, the most majestic of all trees, its branches forming a throne for the clouds to rest upon" (Waters 1963: 51).

Panel C5c
Triangle panels

Twenty-five meters (80 feet) across a broad erosion slope, west of Panel C4, is a large panel facing west. An inverted U-moon high on the rock has a descent path line from the right (east). The main panel section is itemized below.

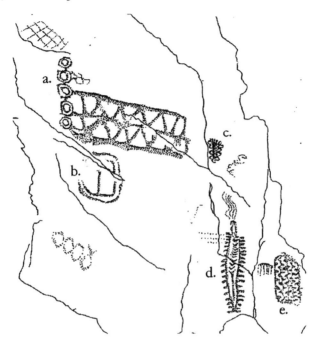

Fig. 8:3

a.	Triangle Panel	Two panels have 4 vertical and 5 inverted triangles; attached to the left are 5 concentric circles. This panel is analyzed as a Venus-sun-moon conjunction related to Area H.
b.	Large split circle	Has been vandalized by over ten bullet holes
c.	Footprint	This footprint has 5 toes and 9 circles around the sides.
d.	Elongated U	There are 18 tics on the left and 19 on the right (37 total); 12 or 13 U-moons on a trail inside.
e.	Box of 4 wavy lines (total 44) and a 6-comb on the side	

This panel is analyzed with other related panels in the Area H Venus-Sun-Moon Conjunctions Section (see page 155). A range of other weathered number tabulations is located in the lower section of the panel.

Panel C6a
Lunar Counts

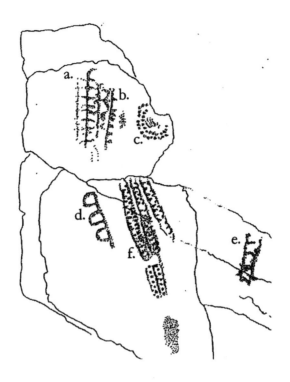

Fig. 8:4

a. Double 8-ladder at upper left = full moon

b. Seven comb = week (1 moon quarter)

c. Double dot circle at upper right chipped area may be 45 day cross-quarter.

d. Three circles on line = 3 moon season

e. Ladder with 4 steps = 4 quarters of the year

f. Three banded wavy lines could be moon cycle (base eroded).

Panel C7a and C7b
Southwest Moon Mother Tradition

Upper end of a west facing boulder has a 14-count ladder for full moon. The Moon Mother (round moon head) at the right has outstretched arms in line with the lunar panel. The Moon Mother in Southwest tradition is symbolic of earth fertility (Waters 1963: 238).

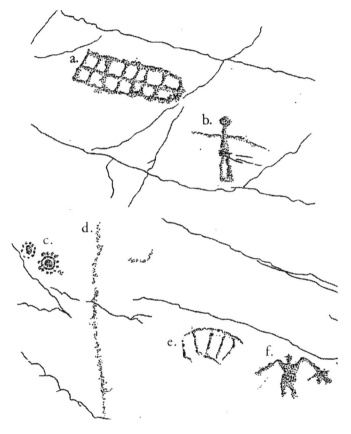

Fig. 8:5

a. Two rows of 7 squares = full moon

b. Moon Mother

c. Ten dot circle and 12 dot circle

d. Vertical trail line

e. Box with 3 sections for a 3-month quarter

f. Human figure with wing shaped arms and large bird talon hand is symbolic of the lunar-solar flight path.

Panel C7c
Migratory Hunting

Fig. 8:6

The footprints are traditional Southwest symbols for nomadic migrations. Two animals and a water fowl at the bottom left and two footprints may relate to migratory hunting. Seasonal dates are marked in the top left 11-comb with other dot counts to the right. The large bear paw has 5 tics at the side (some numbers could be kill tallies). The central section of circles and lines is typical of hunting trail maps. Six circles on a vertical path line turns left to the base to the footprint (hunting foray date).

Panel C8
Migratory Hunting Calendar

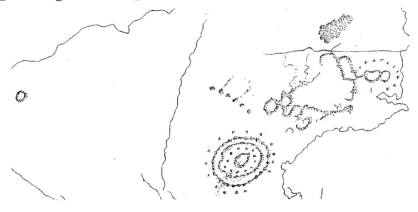

Fig. 8:7

A footprint is over a possible hunting trail map connected to circle locations with calendar or tally dots. A large (20 cm. wide) 3-concentric circle has 12 dots for a full year and 15 dots for a full moon.

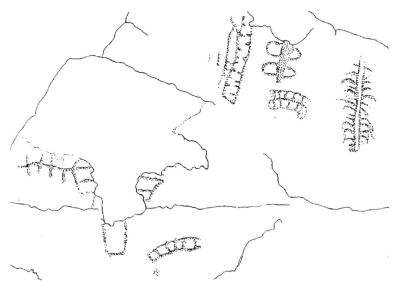

Fig. 8:8

Another section of Panel C8 has a tree with 15 branches on the left and 12 on the right (same counts as concentric sun dots above). At the left are two connected combs with six sections on the bottom and 5 on top. At the left a broad stem has two circles on each side for 4 directional quarters of the year. Other combs and ladders are weathered.

Panel C9
Sun and Moon Counts

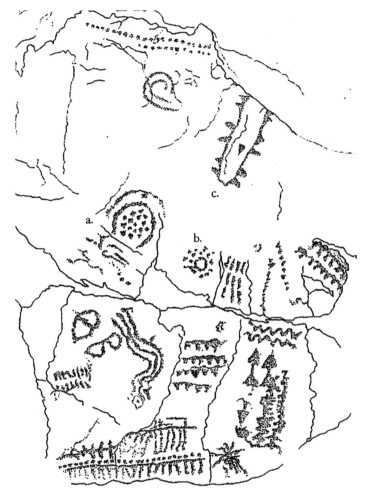

Fig. 8:9

This panel contains a full array of the various count signs: dots, lines, combs, circles, triangles, wavy lines, tic lines, and a triple curved "trail" marker. Weathering around the panel sides has erased complete counts.

    a. This large circle under a crescent line has 16 dots for a full moon count.

    b. Small circle at the right also has 16 dots.

    c. Large oval above has 6 tics on each side for the two 6 month halves of the year.

Panel C10
Gap Observatory Trails

An unusual panel is on a prominent boulder in the center base of the north Gap Narrows slope. The 8 path lines match the east basin observatory cairn sight lines through the Gap for the 8 cross-quarters and 260-day sunset observatory stations. This is also recorded on the 7 horizons and 8 sunsets inside the Narrows on the V–Gap Narrows map (Panel A7).

I found that the Paiute, Ute and Shoshone calendars fit the cross-quarter seasonal calendar we have deciphered at the Gap. The "Council on the Seasons" tales have the seasons starting on the cross-quarters and centered on the solstices and equinox (Smith 1992: 89-91; Palmer 1978: 66–70). The legend, "Why The Moon Changes" and names for lunar phases and seasons reveals a lunar-solar calendar for measuring time by days, quarter months (weeks), months, four seasons, and the year (Palmer 1978: 94–99, 118).

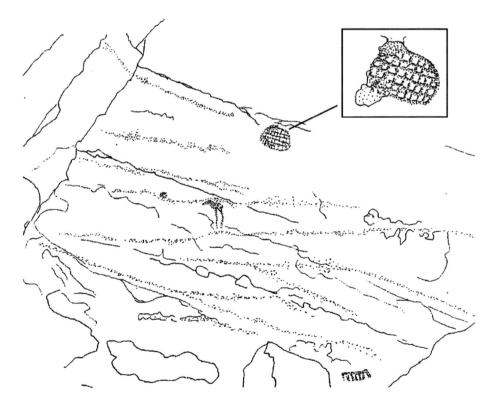

Fig. 8:10

Panel C-10's rock face has:

    a. Top checkered oval is a turtle carapace with 45 sections for a cross-quarter.

    b. Migratory crane stands on the center line facing west toward a setting sun.

    c. Seven long pecked "path" lines (+1 short line) = 8 cross-quarters in a year

    d. Two forked path lines at the bottom suggest the cross-quarter and 260-day calendar cairns in the east basin (Cairn B3 observes both dates through the Narrows—April 29 and May 5; August 5 and August 12).

    e. Seven comb (bottom right) identifies the 7 long path lines above.

Area C Map 2

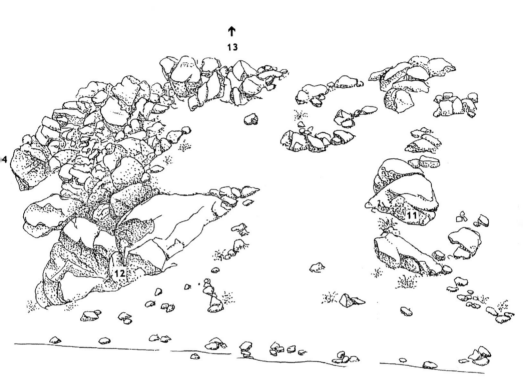

Fig. 8:11—Area C11–C14 Map 2
This section is west of a wide talus slope on the north side.

Panel C11
Tree of Life—Roots and Branches

Panel C11 stands alone near the center of the Gap Narrows emphasizing plant and animal fertility associated with the sun and moon movement through the four seasons. The 7-branch tree of life emphasizes earth fertility and bridging the underworld to the heavens. It relates to other trees in Panels C12, F7b, and the little cave shelter trees oriented to summer season cross-quarter.

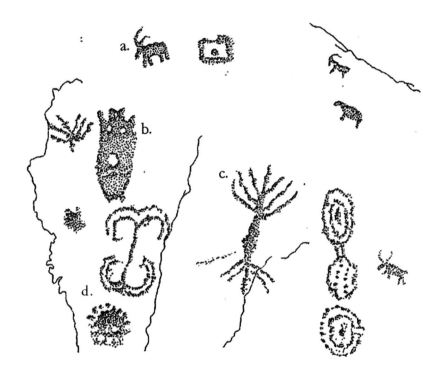

Fig. 8:12

a. Four animals and a square with a dot
b. Female lunar fertility goddess next to 6 branched corn plant
c. 7-branched tree with 5 roots
d. Stylized 4 directional quarter world tree is above a pecked disk with 15 dots for a full moon.

On the right are 3 circles. Top and bottom are concentric seasonal quarters. The three circles symbolize the seasonal structure with equinox midway between the winter and summer solstice. The center circle has two rows of 6 dots for the 2 halves of the year. The outer circle on the bottom contains 20–22 dots for a half cross-quarter.

Panel C12
Sun Circles and Stylized Tree (see Panel C11)

This panel faces the road at the west base of the big talus slope. The figure is extremely weathered from water run off.

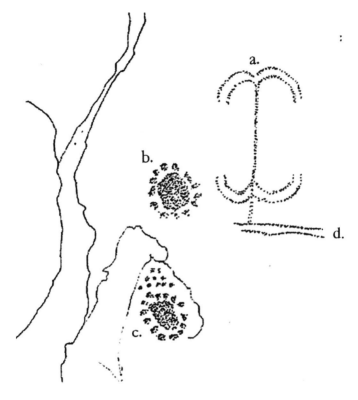

Fig. 8:13

a. Mirrored tree = 4 directional quarter seasons

b. Solid pecked circle with 13 dots = 13 new moons in a year

c. Circle with 14 dots approaches full moon count; other dot count above is weathered

d. Projection of path lines may relate to the Gap pass (compare Panel C10).

Panel C13
Comb, Wheel, and Fremont God

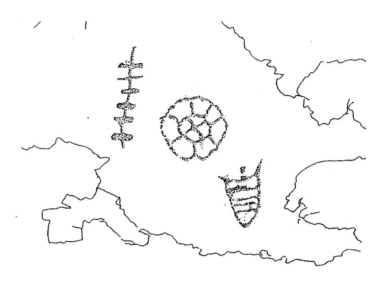

Fig. 8:14

Stand between Areas E and F. Now look up across the road with binoculars to the base of the north peak cliff above the talus slope. The Fremont god figure has a cocoon segmented body like Panel F12's shadow marker for the April 29 sunrise (105–260-day calendar). It points to the year wheel above. The wheel hub divides the year into its four directional quarters of 91 days each (4 × 91 = 364—a year). The outer circle divides the year into 7 sections (7 × 52 = 364 days). This division represents the 105–260-day calendar (see Panel F3 discussion and Parowan Gap Sky Watcher's section). This wheel ties to the adjacent double 6-comb for a year. The significance of this isolated panel high on the north peak relates to another panel oriented to the peak at the cave shelter.

This panel ties to panel G7 at the entrance to the cave shelter. At the upper left of the cave entrance is Panel G7 (see page 153, Fig. 12:4). A large Fremont sky god faces squarely to the Narrows north peak where Polaris sits on top of the peak. I discovered a small stippled disk below the sky god and found it to be a star map of the northern stellar horizon circle (Panel G7 Discussion). The G7 and C13 Panels relate to this annual "star calendar clock"—the annual rotating stars around the Polaris North Star. The wheel has an opening at its base—typical of Southwest design openings for the release of the spirit. The cave opening symbolizes a portal for the passing of the spirit at the time of birth or death with Mother Earth.

Panel C14
Lunar-Solar Counts

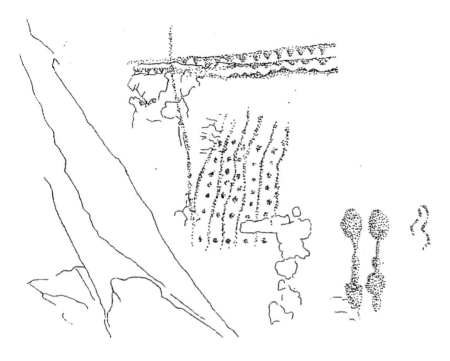

Fig. 8:15

This west facing panel is around the rock corner and above Panel C12. Two short wavy "time cycle" lines at the right label this calendar panel. Two adjacent sun cycle glyphs have a time line between their two circles. The two related cycle counts are recorded above. A box count has five rows of weathered dots. One row has 8 dots so could be 40 or more for a cross-quarter count. A vertical path-line from the box intersects 3 weathered triangle count lines above. The top line has 13 triangles to the right of the path-line. The next line with similar triangle spacing has 3 or 4 to the left of the path-line (4 + 13 = 17). The bottom line has fewer larger triangles that point up to complete another cycle (40 days).

Area D

Fig. 9—Area D Cliffs Map
Area D is located on the west end of the Narrows, north side.

Panel D2a

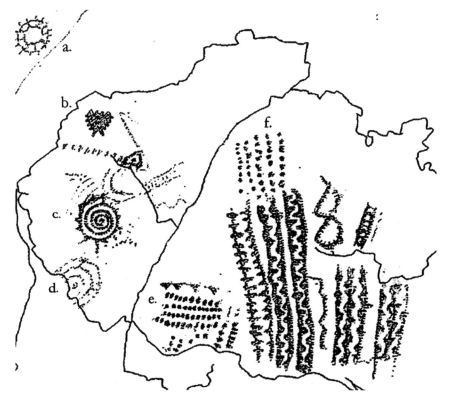

Fig. 9:1—(upper half of Panel D2)
Full Moon and 9-Month Gestation Cycles

Panel D2 is located on a high ledge where the sky watcher had a panoramic view of the western horizon. Large sections of the panel have broken off and left weathered edges. The remaining petroglyphs of over 50 tabulation figures are in rows of dots, lines, ladders, combs, wavy lines, triangle lines, and circle tics. Seven figures at the top left are pictographic:

a. Lunar-Solar Wheel   15 radiant lines for a full moon surround 9 wheel sections (9-month gestation cycle)

b. Bat   A bat ascends by a rock cleft (cave sign?) on a sunset trail line to a sun sitting on 3 dots which are in a line with 9 other dots for the nocturnal gestation cycle of the year (August 12 to April 29) The bat above, as a nocturnal symbol for the underworld, relates to this 9-month winter gestation cycle

c. Moon Counts A crescent moon sitting on a 4+ turn spiral matches the winter solstice (Dec. 21) distance from August 12 to April 29 for the 260-day cycle; the half period of 130 days is 4.4 months, and is recorded in the 12.4 moons in a year (13 new moon tics around the spiral)

d. Concentric

e. The big numbers to the right have some clear counts despite weathering; others approach calendar cycle counts

f. Comb and Dots 4 horizontal rows of dots totaling a 45-day cross-quarter with a 4-comb multiplier above that totals 180 days—a half year

g. Dots and Panel Two wavy line panels are below a box of 41 dots that match dots above the V–Gap map (Panel A7); turns in the two wavy panel below total a cross-quarter; a 15-comb at the side counts a full moon; a double 17-comb (34) is on the left. Other numbers match calendar counts, but most are unclear due to weathering

Panel D2b
Calendar Counts

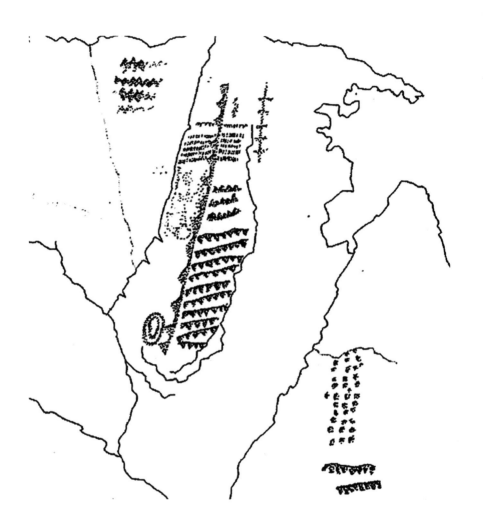

Fig. 9:2—(lower right section of Panel D2)

Extensive counts are grouped around a vertical 13 triangle comb that rises off a concentric circle. Numbers include 13 combs, 10 tic lines (100+) and other dots. The numbers 10 and 13 dominate (10 × 13 = 130 × 2 = 260 fertility cycle?).

Panel D3a
Hunting

Bear hibernation was one facet of tracking migratory animals through their seasonal migrations for hunting. The ancient Fremont recorded measures of time and mapped places of animal migrations, mating seasons, birthing and feeding areas. Recorded details below seem to describe a hunting season.

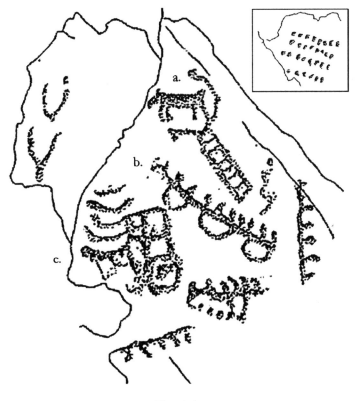

Fig. 9:3

a. Bear Hibernation; a bear in a U-cave at the end of a 7-stepped ladder may record the 7th month from August 12 (start of 260-day gestation cycle) to late February or early March when hibernation ends.

b. Ten tic comb over 3 moon circles records a 30 day month.

c. Left 2 U's and 5 U's by a box are moon signs.

d. A quartered box is over a sun circle for the 4 directional seasons.

e. Other combs have 5–6 teeth.

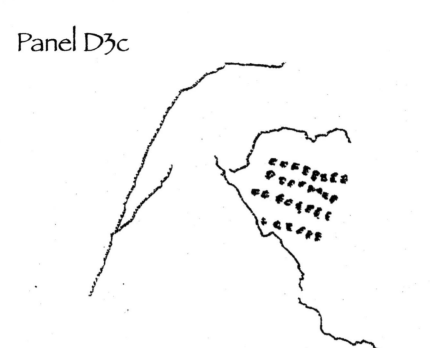

Fig. 9:4
Eight-day quarters for a lunation count (8 + 8 + 8 + 6 = 30)

Panel D6
Sun and Moon Cycles

This is the main panel on a narrow cliff face on the west razor-back ridge. It's commanding position is dominated by a cocoon glyph with major sun and moon cycles.

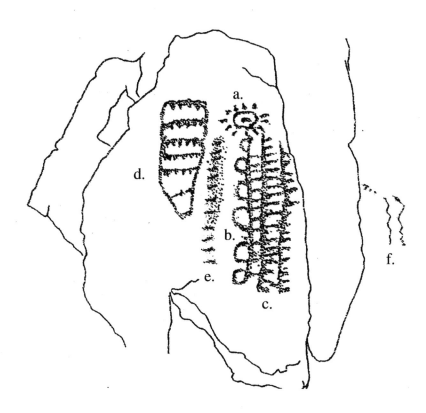

Fig. 9:5

a. Concentric Sun	Twelve rays around a zenith sun count the year months
b. Year Circles Comb	Six moon circles for a solar transit are attached to a 12-comb year sign
c. Moon Cycles Combs	An 18-comb moon may be a lunar Metonic cycle (18.6 years), identified with the attached 15-comb (full moon sign). The two combs also multiply to 9 months (15 × 18 = 270; 9 × 30 = 270). The three combs make a cross-quarter (12 + 18 + 15 = 45)
d. Cocoon Metamorphosis	This commanding cocoon highlights the miracle of insect metamorphosis (recorded on Panel F12, where a year cocoon is an April 29 New-Year shadow marker with a moth-like plant emerging above). This cocoon has to be complimented by the various calendar counts that express complete sun and moon cycles. It has five thorax sections, which is typical of moth and butterfly pupae. Twenty-three tics on the thorax steps equals a half cross-quarter. A tic on a tip step pointing up as a multiplier doubles the count for a 46-day cross-quarter. Between 23 and 46 is an acceptable day range for pupa metamorphosis and emergence during the summer cross-quarter (May 5 to June 21)
e. Year Column	A column of 12 lines next to the cocoon and below the year sun records a completed year cycle for the cocoon metamorphosis
f. Sun-Moon Serpents	Two serpents with 6 body turns (2 halves of year) rise at the right (east) behind 3 dots (quarter sign) toward the zenith sun

Panel D7
Northwest Entrance to the Gap Narrows

A large boulder at the west entrance to the Narrows invites respect and reverence from the traveler passing through the Narrows sacred space. A large saw-tooth panel "mouth" at the top defines this sacred space with two lines of 12 teeth for the year. The sun and moon serpents rise from the jaws as if coming out of a cave mouth. In native tradition, caves and rock fissures are regarded as passage routes for spirits to be released from the interior of the earth related to creation from mother earth. Serpents dwelling in the Narrows rocks often appear through these rock fissures.

In Mesoamerica the spirit's passage routes to sacred space are at times pictured as a serpent or jaguar mouth as a symbolic cave entrance. To the right (east) of this saw-tooth mouth are five triangles for the prime calendar observatory stations (Compare Panels A2 and C5).

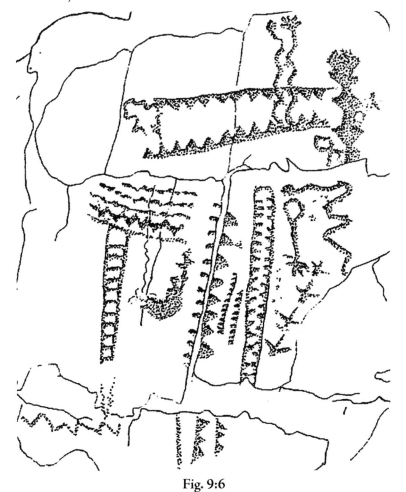

Fig. 9:6

The Narrows figuratively symbolizes the mouth of Mother Earth. The cave shelter inside the Narrows with its many petroglyphs and calendar markers expands this symbolism considerably. The Tobats god head on the cliff face above the cave performs a heirophany with every morning sun throughout the winter season as it can be viewed from the west, swallowing the sun until the February 5 cross-quarter ushers in the spring season for renewed life.

Life renewal in early spring is manifest in nature in a multitude of ways besides plant life. The lower right section of D7 pictures a dramatic life cycle miracle at the Gap. Four geese are pictured flying in their northward migratory flight. Annually 30,000 Snow Geese fly north over the Gap to the Delta marsh lakes during the last two weeks of February. Some birds in the past, when there was water, may have landed at Rush Lake and Little Salt Lake.

The four geese are pictured flying up toward a serpent trail. When I showed the geese migration petroglyph to a friend, Alan Walker, he immediately recognized the snake above the geese as the Sevier River, bending back on its course to Sevier Lake, which is wide at the top and narrow on the south end. Checking the map, the turns and general lengths are consistent, only exaggerated on the petroglyph. The trail off the south end of Sevier Lake is 1.5 times the length of the lake. Before modern irrigation dried up Sevier Lake it had fish and was a migratory bird refuge. A prehistoric campsite was located off the north shore of the lake.

The circle and bird-track trail extending down from the serpent trail head matches Wah Wah Valley due south of Sevier Lake to Sulphur Springs at Lund in the Escalante Desert where trails fork into 4 directions like the birds toes: west to Modena (Mt. Elenore), south to Newcastle (Silver Peaks), and east to Mud Springs (Mud Springs Hill) then southeast as the toe bends to the Parowan Gap—the lower middle dot and line. The location of this map on the boulder at the west end of the Narrows is a complement to the Red Hills map on Panel A10 on the east end of the Narrows. It may similarly be a hunting expedition trail to Sevier Lake to hunt the migratory geese.

Fig. 9:7

Note: Triangle teeth could symbolize the triangle of light seen with the setting sun from the west through V–Gap across the east basin. These triangles of light adapted into this Gap-mouth picture seem to endow sacred space with spirit light.

Area E

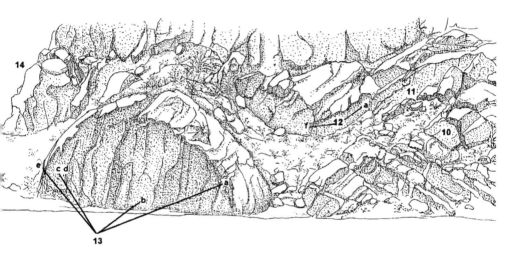

Fig. 10—Area E Cliffs Map
Area E is located on the west end of the Narrows, south side.

Panel E1
Boulder Southwest of Narrows

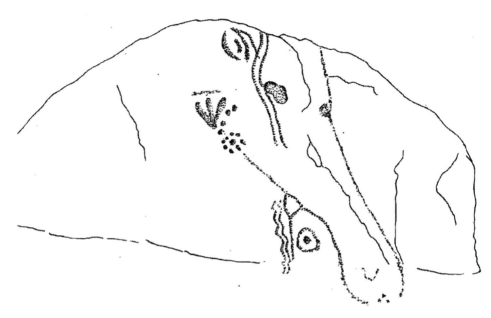

Fig. 10:1 (front)

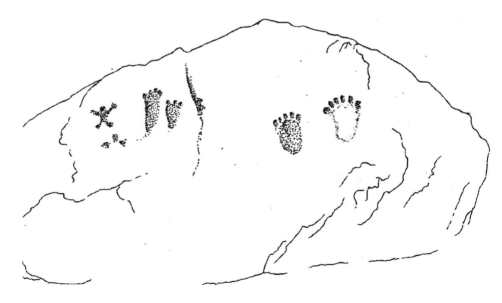

Fig. 10:2 (opposite side)

This large boulder is located just west of the west entrance to the Narrows, on the south field road. It is covered with archaic cupules (cup shaped holes, not drawn). The theme depicted here imitates the D7 bird migration theme. When I excavated this boulder face to expose the erosion cover, a U-basin enclosure was exposed at the base of two converging lines. This revealed a simplified V–Gap map like the Panel A7 V–Gap map. On this panel, 12 dots for the year spiral around a sun circle marking winter solstice at the side of a large ascending bird track below a horizontal line. This depicts the beginning of the snow geese migration northward from their southern winter home. The flight path line is pictured at the right. Three dots below a U-moon at the bottom of the lobe may indicate the 3rd month after the December winter solstice which is the March season for the bird migration pictured on this panel. Two serpents rise on a sun path line on the V–map's left arm.

On the opposite side of the rock (Fig. 10:2) a man with raised arms stands over 3 dots where the viewer following the man's direction will look up to see the migrating geese flying north as recorded on Boulder D7. Perhaps the footprints (pointing up with 3, 4, 5, and 6 toes) symbolize the many who gathered to watch the annual snow geese migrations and perhaps participate in the migration hunt.

Panel E2
Footprints Boulder

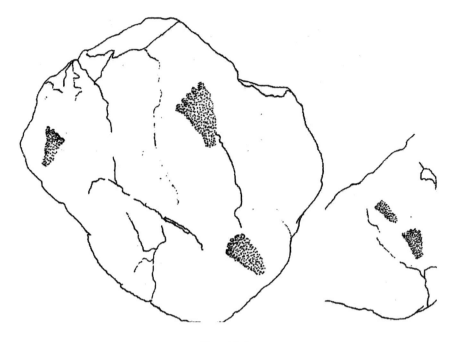

Fig. 10:3

The boulder near E1 has five foot prints in progressive sizes (10, 12, 17, 20, 28 cm.). The largest matches an adult man's size 10 foot. The smallest narrow foot closely matches a 3-year-old boy's foot.

This boulder belongs to a large campsite that once had grinding stones, tools, and Fremont ceramic shards. I like to think the foot print boulder was left by a family that once camped here and recorded their footprints on the "sandstone of time" for future generations. All footprints are ascending. Footprints symbolize travel, migration or hunting trails.

Panel E10
Lunar–Solar 12 Month Year

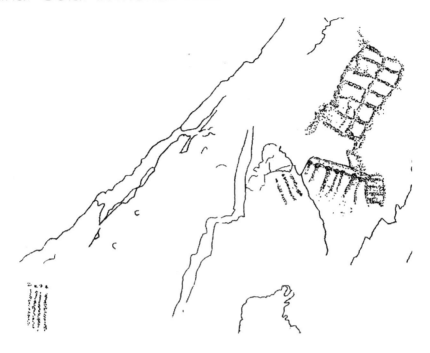

Fig. 10:4

This is the first panel located inside the Narrows, beyond a recess in the rocks east of a small cave shelter visible near the road. It has typical Gap calendar figures.

a. A double ladder at the top records the two 6-month halves of the year as it moves on two bottom legs from June 21 and December 21 solstices; the tapering ladders show the relative changing day lengths from summer solstice (left) and winter solstice (right) to equinox at the top

b. A moon cycle glyph is attached below the winter solstice right leg; a 7-day comb for a moon-quarter is doubled across the top for full moon; a 4-box is attached to the right side for the 4 quarters of the month; three left lines may be 3 moon quarters; four more dot lines to the lower left match the 4 season quarters

Two other figures detached (not pictured) at the lower right of this panel continue with moon cycle counts. This is one of many panels at the Gap that focuses on the 9-month human fertility-gestation cycle. A moon circle is divided into 9-month sections with path lines below. To the lower right are 19 dots for a lunar Metonic cycle (see Panel B3a).

Panel E11
Moon Signs

Fig. 10:5

Dim and weathered symbols are on a high narrow ledge above Panel E10. The three figures in the drawing are more separated on the long panel. Crescents are consistently moon signs with spiral turns symbolizing lunation counts.

Left Spiral Plant	3 spirals reverse to an outer crescent (compare Little Salt Lake Panel J1). The spiral rises off a plant with 5 stems on one branch
Crescent Moon	A double crescent moon has 6 dots for 6 months
Plant	A corn plant has 6 leaves for a possible half year count (see Panel C11)

Below are 3 lines attached to a moon circle by a dot

Panel E12

A variety of weathered figures indicate an extended time period for this long panel located along east of Panel 11 (not visible from the road).

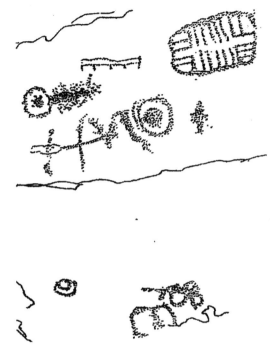

Fig. 10:6

Sunwatcher	A human figure faces a concentric sun passing on a path line through the V–Gap to a horizon line sunset; the sunset date is recorded above with a double comb attached to the sun (weathered) under a 5-comb
Oval Year Record	Four corner boxes relate to the four cardinal directions and four seasons. Oval is split for 2 halves of the year with 6 spaces (5 lines) on each side for the 6 month halves of the year
Moon Signs	Moons signs at the bottom include a new moon crescent circle, an inverted moon descending on its path line, and 3 moon circles on a path line

Panel E12d and E12e

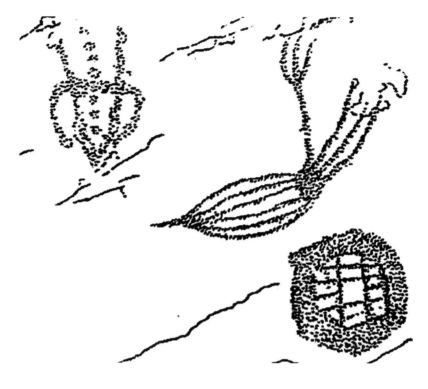

Fig. 10:7

Squash	A squash has 4 vines in 3 sections = year quarters; the numbers relate to the 3-month growing season to August harvest
Year Circle	Four steps in three sections = year quarters; five steps in 3 sections = 15 (full moon)

These calendar numbers appear to relate to three or four month periods in the agriculture planting/harvest season

V–Moon	(Located farther left) A V–dagger with 8 days for a moon quarter cuts through a moon crescent; the dagger indicates the increasing light with the moon quarter progression

Panel E13

This is the largest and most ideal and accessible rock panel in the Gap, but strangely has only four isolated figures plus a Spanish and a historic section.

Fig. 10:8

Fremont God

A split triangle torso on one leg is lightly pecked and appears to be an unfinished Fremont god figure; it is located at the far right and is not duplicated elsewhere at the Gap; a lightly pecked 4-quarter unfinished box is at the bottom center of the panel.

Fig. 10:9

God's Spiral Eye

This is a realistic eye with pupil and 12 eye lashes (12 months), composed around a 2-turn spiral (2 lunations); it is the one well executed figure on the main panel face, and is located on the east edge keeping a "protective watch."

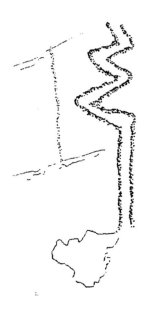

Fig. 10:10

Trail Line   A double lined wavy path on the east facing side of the panel appears to be a trail path.

Panel E's location at the base of a possible ritual access route through the cliffs to the south peak should also be noted. Around the corner on an east facing rock side is a vertical path with 5 turns on the upper half. Testing this as a possible path map, I ascended up through the rocks to the left and climbed on west. After five switchbacks along ledges during the ascent through the cliffs, I was able to climb to the top of the south peak where I located a Vision Quest site oriented to summer solstice sunrise.

Fig. 10:11

The cross bones box with the 1939 date overlaps an earlier deeply pecked Spanish Cross (compare B11a Spanish Cross). These are the earliest recorded historic dates at the Gap that are fortunately limited.

Panel E14
Sheep

Fig. 10:12

This rare isolated sheep is located in a recess where sheep entering the Gap could rest in the rocks or be cornered and ambushed. This might have been a spring "birthing" spot for sheep. A round "pregnant" sheep has a dot at its tail and another in front and may relate to Panel F2 that celebrates the full moon (time of birthing). The 5 dots above may identify completion of the gestation cycle depicted on Panel F3. The sheep has sky-heaven associations in Southwest legends.

Area F

Fig. 11—Area F Cliffs Map
Area F is located at the center of the Narrows, south side.

Area F starts in the center cliffs and extends eastward into a large, well protected recessed area with good morning sun and afternoon shade, a welcome gathering place from the warm summer sun. This may account for the 150+ petroglyphs pecked here. Erosion and re-pecking indicates a long history in the petroglyphs which challenges de-coding them. Test excavations exposed some petroglyphs covered by soil erosion. A heavy rock and boulder fall on the east has buried some petroglyphs. A large boulder in the cave shelter, probably from an earthquake, buried a first century A.D. occupation level and petroglyphs nearly three thousand years older (3000 B.C.). There is a lot of duplication of calendar figures here, but also interesting innovations.

Panel F1

Fig. 11:1

The west end of Area F begins with an isolated box composed of 5 vertical lines. This is a common glyph for the five divisions of the sun's transit between winter and summer solstice. It is directly opposite the north peak. The figure forms 4 cross-quarters in the half year between the solstice signs, which matches the observatory cairns.

Panel F2
Lunar

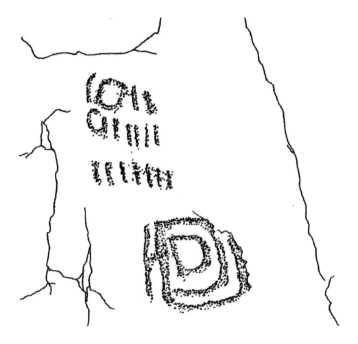

Fig. 11:1

This panel at the top of the narrow talus slope records the moon progression from new-moon crescent at the bottom to quarter moon (half circle) with two 7-day quarter counts above leading to full moon (15 days) at the top. This narrow slot would have been illuminated by full moon overhead as night settled in, and may have had a ceremonial role with the moon's fertility tie to mother earth as in traditional Native American beliefs.

Panel F3
260-Day, 9-Month Sacred Calendar

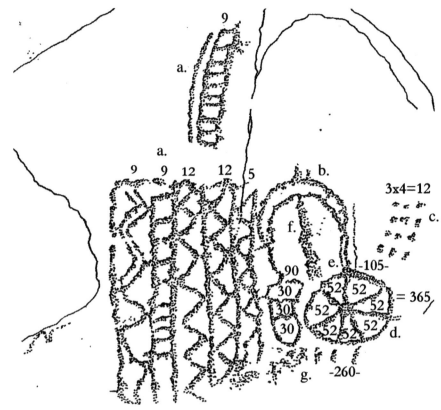

Fig. 11:2

Panel F3 is located at the base of the cliff near the corner where the talus slope rises to F2. Drainage water has eroded the base of this panel. This panel is composed of five columns of waves, circles and a ladder. Calendar signs are:

a. Two 9-ladders (9 moons) emphasize the 260-day fertility-pregnancy cycle

b. Geometric design with an umbrella over a wheel; this relates to the sky canopy on Panel F7a and Panel 7b

c. Box of 12 dots above the wheel = year (4 rows of 3 dots for 4, 3-month seasons)

d. Seven-spoke year wheel is 7 × 52 = 364 days in the 260-day (5 × 52 = 260 days) and 105-day (2 × 52 = 104 days); Panel C13 on the north peak cliff matches this wheel

e. Wheel top = summer solstice with path lines connecting to a new moon crescent; another path line extends down from the left side of the moon to a 3-section oval

f. A bold line from the middle of the crescent connects down to the August 12 beginning of 9-month, 260-day calendar

g. Five dots below the wheel also identify these five sections in the 260-day cycle

The isolated location of this important panel can be explained in two ways. It may belong to an observation station here to view winter cross-quarter sunrise on the distant horizon against the Narrows cliff. It was probably selected as the place of symbolic emergence from mother earth at the corner of the long fissure in the cliff where Panel F2 at the top is dedicated to new moon birth.

Panel F4
Calendar Plot

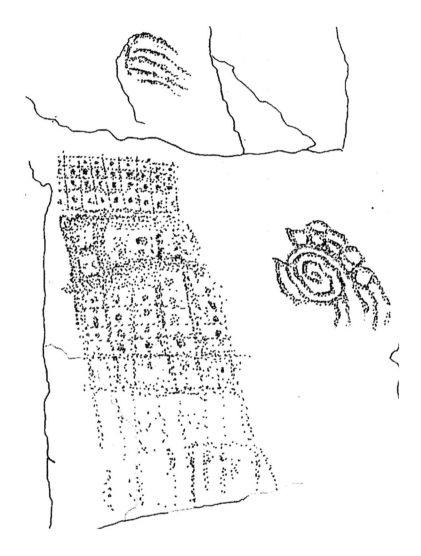

Fig. 11:3

High on a cliff ledge above Panel F3 is a large weathered checkerboard box of squared dots with 3 different size sections. Counts appear to be 6 × 20 = 180 days (half year). Equinox observatory Cairn E1 splits the year in half (182 + 182 = 364 days), then splits again at the solstices into four 91-day quarters (see Calendar Wheel).

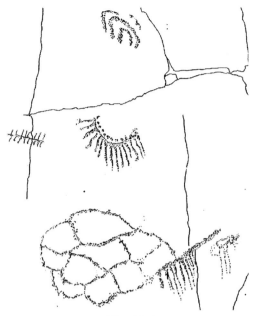

Fig. 11:4

Moon figures above the large panel include a 15-comb crescent with 12 or 13 dots in the crescent for a year count. An inverted U-moon is above and a double lunar quarter-comb is at the left. At the bottom is a cluster of 10 circles resting on a comb.

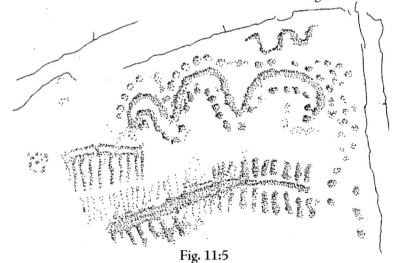

Fig. 11:5

The other panel section to the lower right has a long double comb at the bottom and another comb and dotted circle to the left. The main figure is a wavy line with 45 dots across the top and to the right side for a cross-quarter. There are 20 dots along the base of the wave. A 4-turn wave above may be a multiplier. These numbers combine to plot the 260-day cycle ($45 + 20 = 65 \times 4 = 260$).

Panel F5
Sky Watcher's Calendar Record

Over a hundred dots are on this panel that is weathered by erosion. The lower excavated section is well preserved by an erosion cover. Dot totals are uncertain.

a. Five rows of 9 dots = 45 cross-quarter count

b. Above a human face is a bar-bell with 6 dots to the right; the bar-bell is a cycle glyph and the dots indicate a 6-month cycle; this may be a sign for the sky watchers record

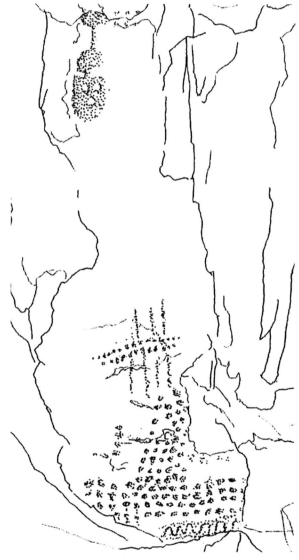

Fig. 11:6

Panel F7
Cosmic Heavenly Journey

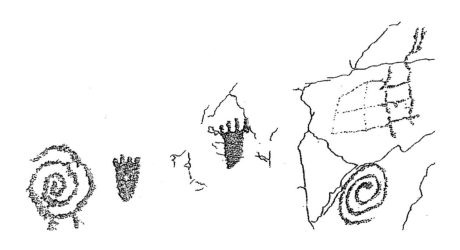

Fig. 11:7

A high petroglyph panel rises to the highest possible reach. The ascent path is marked by two separate foot prints. Both have 4 toes as a sign of the cosmic journey recorded here through the four seasons. This journey is also indicated by a moon circle on the lower foot, which is by a prominent 3-turn moon spiral (20 cm. wide) for a quarter. It stands on two legs as a sign for its journey through the three month quarter-season. The two legs may double for a half year. This record is confirmed at the top where another 3-turn spiral is set under a box with two rows of 3 squares for the two quarters in a half year. Thus, the foot and spiral at the first rise step set the stage for the detailed cosmic journey above.

Panel F7a
Cosmic Tree

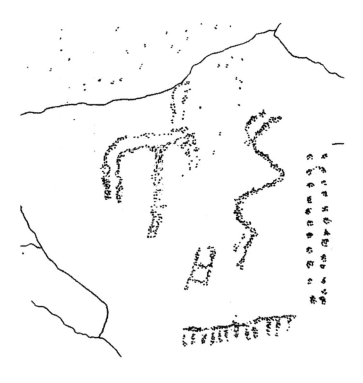

Fig. 11:8

The climb reaches a high point on the cliff (F7a) where a two branched tree forms a sky canopy with a path rising off the tree top into a starry sky of stipple star dots. It is next to a "numbers" serpent (4 body turns, 2 mouth jaws) with a 12-comb and a 3-step moon ladder below identifying the year and it's quarters. The serpent numbers as multipliers point to two parallel dot lines.

- One has 11 dots, possibly for cross-quarter cycles (4 × 11 = 44 (45) × 2 = 90-day quarter)
- The other line has 13 dots, possibly for the 52-day cycle divisions and summer season (4 × 13 = 52 × 2 = 104-day summer)

This is an abbreviated record from the A10 serpent calendar panel on the cliff across the Narrows. These same dot-line numbers are repeated above another mirrored tree at the upper left with 2 and 4 numbers (F7b described below).

Panel F7b
Four Seasons and 260-Day Calendar

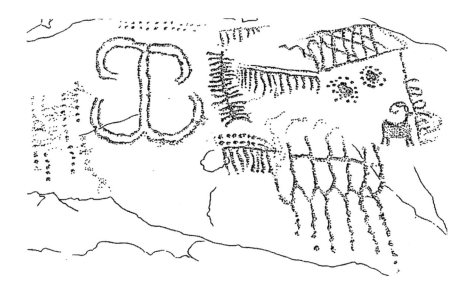

Fig. 11:9

The dominant glyph on the left side is a large 4-quarter geometric figure with adjacent weathered dot lines. It's 4-quarter circular branches extend off the central trunk. The trunk and top canopy match the tree in F7a. We can now recognize this as the same canopy tree on Panel F3 that ties to the summer growing season wheel. This mirrored tree with added elements is found inside the cave shelter (see Panel G2) where it more clearly pictures the two halves of the year with its 3-month, 4-quarter seasons.

The different figures in this section record the journey through sun and moon cycles marked by dots, dotted circles, combs, and a double comb (year). Starting at the top right, a lattice panel compares to the H1 and H3 Venus panels. A sheep stands against a 9-tooth comb (gestation cycle) attached below the lattice. Below the back of the sheep a curious geometric design may record the year with a 6 + 12 pattern. Six lines extending down have weathered dotted ends. To the left is a 9-comb that has two rows of 9 dots along the comb's back. These 9 numbers tie through the geometric year glyph to the sheep and its 9-comb to emphasize the fertility gestation cycle. At the top center are three combs with lunar cycle counts—week, full moon, month and 13 moon year.

Panel F10
Moon Journey Record

The remainder of the lower south cliff in Area F was recorded in three panels and 13 drawings of figures that are mostly repetitious. So we will focus on the panel sections that add new information.

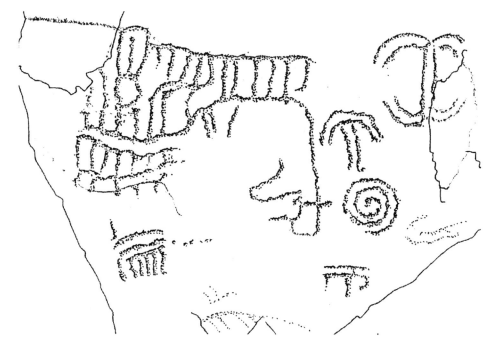

Fig. 11:10

This panel may be a pictograph for describing the moon's cycles and day counts. The large ladder at the top expanding left (east) matches the moon's progression from new moon appearance in the western sky (right side) represented by a crescent "new moon" line at the far right end of the ladder. Fifteen day lines expand left to a full moon circle, with a split loop on top for the two halves of the lunation. The top line continues left (east) and disappears into a crack in the cliff, suggesting the last crescent moon's disappearance in the eastern sky before new moon. A small companion ladder below the left side of the big ladder has a similar left expansion for a quarter moon progression of 7 days. Two lines at its upper right may record two quarters to full moon, and another line at the side could be a repeat for the second half quarters. Thirteen lines across the bottom of the big ladder match the 13 moons in a year.

The right new moon crescent appears to rise above a meandering path line as if emerging from the underworld. This meandering line is a continuation of the bottom line of the big lunation ladder, so may represent the new moon's return to the western sky through the underworld, as described in traditional beliefs. It could also relate to the moon's setting in the west and progressive underworld journey following the sun's daily setting.

Four separate figures at the right side record moon cycles in a 3-turn spiral above a 3-comb for the 3-month quarter. The crescent tree above pictures the moon's path across the sky and with a "tree" trunk may signify cosmic growth through the four seasons signified in the quartered tree at the right (compare Panel F7).

Panel F10b

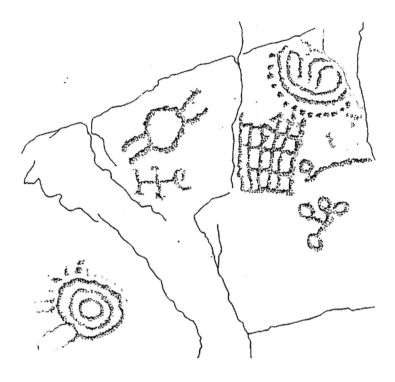

Fig. 11:11

This panel section continues left (east) on Panel 10b to complete the second half of a lunation from full moon. The crescent at the top with 15 dots points up and slightly right like the last moon crescent on the eastern horizon. The moon's ends collapse with the disappearing moonlight. A checkered box below records moons last half (3 × 5 = 15 days). An adjacent down curving path has a moon circle on its left (east) descent end. Four circles below picture the 4 quarter moon phases. The same record is in a moon at the upper left with 4 attached lines for the 4 quarters. A 3-concentric sun circle for a 3-month quarter has weathered dots and sun rays. The visible section can project a 30 day month count (see Panel G2).

Panel F10d

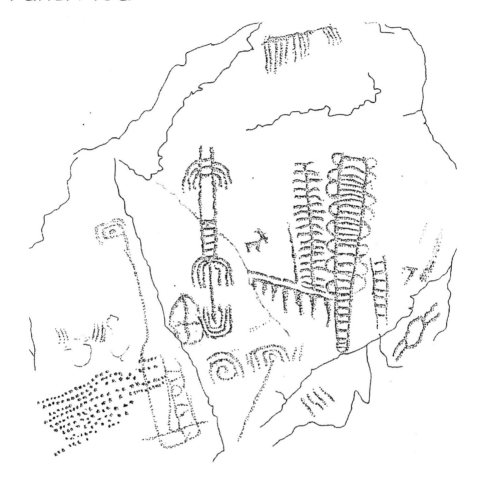

Fig. 11:12

This panel is oriented east and has a summer solstice shadow interaction. The little sheep in the center is a focal point for the calendar signs. A trail line below the sheep moves from a crack line along an expanding 7-day count-comb from new moon to a half moon circle at the right end (quarter moon). The trail rises in front of the sheep along a double 18 plant-like comb (7 + 18 + 18 = 43 for a cross-quarter). This path was created from a shadow line at summer solstice (Fig. 11:14). The ladder and path point up to a 13-comb at the top of the panel; the path aligns perfectly to the comb's left tooth. I found this comb interacts with a summer solstice midmorning shadow line that descends to the ladder below. The comb has 13 teeth for a full year. Nine teeth on the left relate to the southern 260-day fertility cycle. In summary, the sheep's trail appears to rise from the summer cross-quarter to the summer solstice comb shadow marker at the top.

The large tapering ladder records the lunation from new moon at the base through 30 day steps. The 8 moon circles at the sides represent the moon quarters in a lunation. The 7-step ladder at the right side is another quarter sign.

The large geometric tree behind the sheep is deeply grooved (compare 4-branched figure in the cave panel (G2). Its branches with the mirrored base records the four 3-month seasons at the ends of the solar transit trunk, like the other trees (Panels F7, F10). The tree extension at the top is a repeat with 6 steps in the trunk ladder base replacing the curved branches.

Adjacent figures at the base confirm the tree's symbolic calendar meaning. A lightly pecked cross-circle labels the four quarters in the tree. A 3-turn spiral below confirms the 3-month quarter. An adjacent 3-concentric U on a moon-rise path pictures the 3-month quarter like a 3-concentric circle at the top of another long path (upper left). The large field of dots at the lower left is too weathered to get an accurate count, but does approach a half year (182 days).

Fig. 11:13

Panel F11

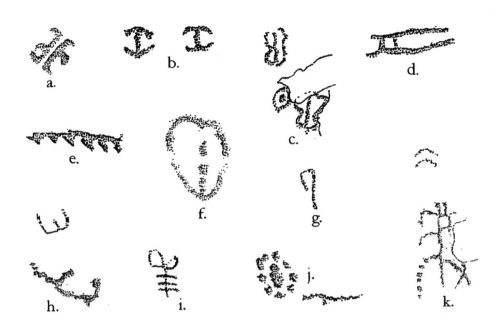

Fig. 11:14
This is a composite of scattered figures from 7 different drawings.

Following the F12 New Year panel east, scattered, isolated figures introduce the extensive south petroglyph gallery. These figures are like lecture notes introducing the basic structures of the lunar-solar calendar. I can picture initiates being brought here for that purpose, going through the following figures:

a. Two E signs, back to back, form a pictograph of the sun's rise from winter solstice (left) through equinox to summer solstice (right), then back again; equinox marks the 4 seasons.

b. Curved ends on two other lines similarly picture solstice turning on the 4-quarter seasons.

c. Two circles split by a line also show quarters for the two halves of the year between the solstices; the larger top relates to longer summer days; a concentric sun at the side labels the sun's path.

d. Horizontal ladder with two steps introduces the moon-count ladder; the two lines may also relate to the moons west and east paths.

e. A 6-saw-tooth comb records a half year.

f.   Three dots in a circle is a 3-month quarter sign; the tapered base is winter solstice.

g.   Inverted U on trail up high (compare B1c, C5a) pictures the moon's last phase descent east.

h.   Two other U's with trail lines relate to the moon's movement.

i.   Another U has a trail line made into a double 3-comb for two 3-month quarters (half year).

j.   Circle with 9 dots by a trail leading west through the Gap measures 9 months (gestation).

k.   Humanoid moon lunation (described below).

The humanoid lunation relates the four limbs to the moon's four quarters. The moon crescent legs stand out with the left one forming a 7-dot quarter count. The right leg has a crescent new moon on the western rise path. Both legs complete the two quarters to full moon at the head. The crescent arms by the moon head picture the natural descent on the left (east) side through the last two quarters. Crescent horns may indicate the two halves of a lunation or the last two quarters in the arms. Two crescents overhead label this lunation figure.

Panel F11c

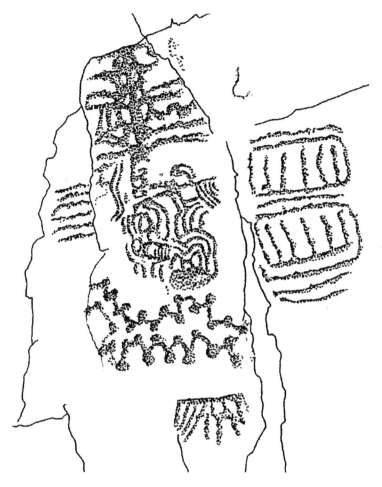

Fig. 11:15

Two irregular 8-sawtooth lines (15–16 sides) have dots at each turn for the two halves of a full lunation. These dots confirm a count system with each turn of a saw-tooth or wavy line. This is a key to reading these wavy lines at the Gap. An interesting geometric figure to the right has two matching boxes divided into 6 sections, obviously for the two 6-month halves of the year. Lines above, between, and below relate to equinox and solstices. The lower box, instead of being closed, opens into a spiral that crosses the bottom and turns up the left side. I believe this sign relates to the solstice turning to the next 6-month box above. Upper middle complex of figures is indistinct.

Panel F12
New Year Shadow Marker Cocoon

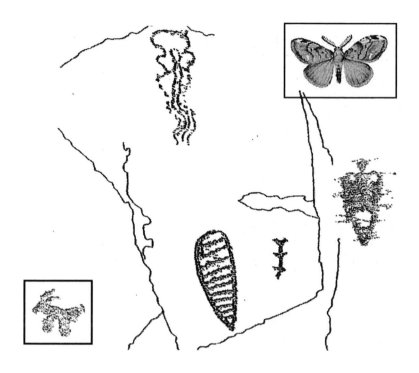

Fig. 11:16

Strangely there are no petroglyphs on the cliffs for 20 meters west of the cave shelter. I discovered that the closest one is a remarkable sun shadow that pinpoints a specific date at the moment of sunrise on April 29 and August 12. A cocoon shaped ladder is illuminated on its left side. The point of the cocoon comes off a recess in the cliff, as if from the cave to signify birth from the underworld. Twelve steps symbolize 12 months The shadow line also silhouettes a path line or plant above. This figure compares favorably to moth wings (figure inset) so we may be viewing a moth or butterfly emerging in metamorphosis on the flight path above the cocoon.

As the sun rises, the shadow crosses the cocoon and bends into a pointer at the 8th step where the 105-day summer season concludes on the sun's return date of August 12. These are the only days in the year when this figure is fully illuminated at sunrise. After the shadow pointer, the rising sun continues to move the shadow line to the right where it silhouettes a curved figure, halts, and then recedes. I believe this figure is a humanoid corn plant to represent both plant and human fertility growth during this summer season. The marvel of the summer season of life starts with an emergence from an underworld cocoon, as from the cliff recess. A goddess around the cliff corner from the plant presides. A Fremont mother goddess shaped like the cocoon rises with breasts and womb circles as symbols of her earth fertility (compare C13 cocoon god and D6 cocoon calendar).

Panel F12c

Fig. 11:17

An isolated big horn sheep (Fig 11:17) is in the middle of a large vacant panel east of the cocoon new year petroglyph. The ball legs suggest the sheep accompanies solar travel through its seasonal cycles. This has a symbolic tie to the sheep's migration and fertility-gestation cycle. This figure could highlight the importance of the 260-day cycle on the cocoon glyph heading the calendar petroglyphs at the east end of Area F (similarly represented on the V–lobe calendar Panel 7 in Area A).

Area G

Shelter 42In37 Unit B

Shelter 42In37 Unit A

Fig. 12—Area G Cliffs Map
Area G is located in the east end of the Narrows, south side.

Panels G2–G9
Cave Shelter Excavation and Shrine Petroglyphs Cultural History

Fig. 12:1
Author excavating cave shelter

The Parowan gap cave shelter with its many petroglyphs functioned as a ritual shrine spanning millennia within the extensive Narrows petroglyph archive. This discovery came to light during the ten year archaeological project (1993–2003) involving field survey, excavation, petroglyph recording, archaeo-astronomy, and comparative ethnography (traditions) research.

Extensive vandal digging over many years destroyed most of the cave shelter's occupation floor deposits. Our crew was fortunate to locate an untouched section after removing looters backfill in 1994, which we excavated in 1996 and 1997. Whatever artifact treasures might have been pilfered cannot match the treasures of knowledge recovered from our excavation that exposed nearly 5,000 years of history at the Gap.

This little cave doubtless provided temporary shelter for some travelers, but its limited space and possible taboos could have discouraged most casual campers. Deep ash deposits from fire pits throughout 500 years of Fremont history in Parowan Valley may have accumulated mainly from sky watchers studying the stars at the Gap as they recorded their observations on the cliffs and performed seasonal rituals.

The most exotic artifact excavated was a little stone animal head broken from a bear effigy. Other Fremont artifacts include ceramic shards, a few stone grinding tools, and Parowan basal notched points. Lithic flakes and bone were throughout the excavation fill. Charcoal from fire pits provided Carbon 14 dates for the different stratigraphic periods.

A single fire pit above sterile deposits after the Fremont abandonment dated to about A.D. 1350. A Desert Side Notched point from this pit, not found previously, revealed this as a Numic (Paiute) camp. Deep ash deposits spanned Fremont history from about A.D. 700 to 1250. Fremont ceramics at several camp sites in the Gap area, including five with petroglyphs, tell the same story. The Parowan Valley villages were major players here during five centuries of Fremont history.

A probable earthquake caused a boulder to fall into the cave and bury an early first century A.D. floor. It rested inches away from weathered petroglyphs at the floor level, so I knew they had to be much older. What was most surprising, as I reached into the narrow opening and cleaned the rock to check for petroglyphs (see Panel G2b) I found weathered petroglyphs like many others among the Fremont petroglyphs. These include concentric suns, a moon circle above a tabulation box by a bird track, and line counts and trial lines by a deer or sheep track (see Panel G2b below).

These figures were already heavily weathered when the boulder fell closing off this area that would have been completely covered by soil erosion. The Fremont also leveled the floor over the boulder. So how old are these petroglyphs? I sank a test pit in June 1997 into a narrow opening between the boulder and front wall down through sandy erosion with charcoal mix, probably re-deposited over centuries of seasonal drainage through the Narrows.

At a depth of 45 cm., I hit a fire pit with burnt stone and bone. A charcoal sample gave a C14 date back nearly 5,000 years. So these petroglyphs could have been over 3,000 years old when the Fremont arrived about 1,300 years ago. This speaks volumes for the longevity and continuity of Native American cultures here. Fremont village dwellers adopted and adapted earlier petroglyphs, assimilating Archaic hunter gathering peoples. So we must remain tentative in judging what is and is not Fremont in origin. Without question, the three or four earlier turtle carapace petroglyphs in the lower cave panel, and one outside (G1) were adopted and adapted. The upper edge of the large top turtle on G2 may have been chipped off when the rock above was prepared for the Fremont panel, but it could still have been used by the early Fremont along with the lunation circle at its left, which was copied for a similar lunation circle above. An early date for the bottom moon circle and adjacent turtle is favored. The concentric circle (bottom left) records a full moon in the spokes and a full lunation in 30 dots. It is unique at the Gap and compares most closely to megalithic petroglyphs at Newgrange, Ireland dated to 3300 B.C.. (Hadingham 1985: 51). A 3,000 B.C. date projected for the Gap circle raises an intriguing question of possible ancient cultural contact.

The bigger picture of the cave's external relations emerged as distant cairns were found to be located where they would interact astronomically with the cave. These include two summer solstice sunset cairns (A1, A3) and two winter solstice sunrise cairns (H1, H2). I found a dramatic heirophany from Cairn A1 where the sun appears to set into the cave bench "roof" at summer solstice. Minutes later a sliver of light off the sun's right edge illuminates the eye and mouth recesses of the Tobats god mask carved by nature into the cliff above the cave. This mask identified as the creator god Tobats by a Paiute informant, could have been inherited from the Fremont, or the tradition could go back to Archaic ancestors of the Paiute who influenced the Fremont. This intriguing question must be left to future research.

Sunrise petroglyph interactions from two observatory gnomons inside the cave clinch both the summer solstice and 260–105-day summer season celebrations. The latter is most dramatic. A sunlight dagger tip settles perfectly into a small petroglyph wedge on April 29–30 at the end of the cosmic circle and spiral petroglyphs to celebrate completion of the spring birth season. The light dagger returns again to its wedge on August 12–13 at the end of the 105-day summer growing season to initiate the 260-day fertility gestation cycle which goes to winter solstice and back to complete another birth cycle the next spring (April 29). There can be no more important and precisely dated calendar celebration of life at the Gap than this.

A standing stone inside the cave was notched on top forming a gnomon marker that projects summer solstice sunrise to the cave's back wall.

Everything we have learned about the cave as a temple portal to the spirit world in Southwest and Mesoamerican cosmology finds expression in the Gap cave. This cave is the equivalent of the Pueblo kiva, and the subterranean cave beneath the Pyramid of the Sun at Teotihuacan, Mexico or the tomb beneath the pyramid temple at Palenque, Mexico with their passageways to the underground spirit world. Numerous Maya temple sanctuaries similarly portray the temple portal entry as a god mask mouth, variously pictured as a snake or jaguar mouth passage to and from the spirit world in the heavens and the underground. The Gap petroglyphs provide a rich record on cave symbolism. Discussion of the petroglyphs in the main Panel G3 follows.

Area G, isolated from Area F, focuses on the Cave Shelter and adjacent petroglyphs.

Two figures isolated in a recess at the base of the cliff near the cave shelter (42 In37) bridge the cave across a 25 meter cliff void to petroglyphs in Area F. A turtle carapace 20 cm. high related to others in the cave (Figs. G2, G6b) signifies emergence from the underworld through a rock cleft. A date recorded on its back ties to the turtle coming out of winter hibernation with spring renewal. Faint lines on the weathered top reveals 12 original steps. Parallel lines in the three sections can be reconstructed as three 12-week or 3-month seasons for the 9-month gestation cycle to spring birth. This ties nicely to the 260-day calendar shadow markers on

Fig. 12:2—Panel G1

panel F12 and also in the cave shelter for the April 29–30 completion date.

The calendar figure at the bottom is a variation of the year glyph on Panel F11c, and confirms that the same people carved both figures—the people who preserved the blank cliff stretch in between. Accordingly, this untouched cliff is part of the sacred space related to emergence from the underworld to celebrate New Year with the panel F12 shadow marker that marks the beginning of the summer growing season April 29–30.

Figure G1b   Is two early historic names without dates on a cliff ledge above. The lower name is weathered away except for a few faint letters. The upper name is Joseph Dalton who belonged to the Dalton family among the early settlers at Parowan.

Introduction to Figures G2–G9, Cave Shelter 42In37

Numerous weathered petroglyphs are found inside the cave shelter (A) recorded in 6 panels, and in its annex (B) recorded in 3 panels. The cave shelter has a distinctive function within the Narrows petroglyph site. Shelter A emphasizes geometric and numerical figures. If the extensive Fremont occupation of the shelter, evident in deep ash deposits, was involved in hunting forays, it does not show up in the shelter petroglyphs. There are no game animal figures. In contrast, there are two mammals and a half dozen deer tracks in the little annex Shelter B (Fig. G9c). An Archaic section at the base of the main panel (G2a) does have one distinct deer track among calendar glyphs, and a large bird talon. I believe the answer to the absence of game animals lies in the major activity at the Narrows as a sacred calendar ritual site, and that cave Shelter A was the focus of the spirit world with its deep inner narrow corridor.

While the cave doubtless provided shelter for the traveler on occasion, its major function for the Parowan Valley Fremont was primarily concerned with ritual activities for agricultural and animal fertility. Petroglyphs and observatory functions at the Gap imply ritual activities were scheduled with lunar and solar observations on key calendar dates, also observed from the cave and recorded on its walls. This implies to me religious ritual supplications much like Southwest Pueblo Indians practice today in annual rain dances. I also believe this natural sacred role of the cave shelter was recognized from the earliest times, and was respected and preserved through time, just as Paiutes today tend to avoid the shelter because of traditional beliefs.

Panel G2
Cave Shelter Petroglyphs

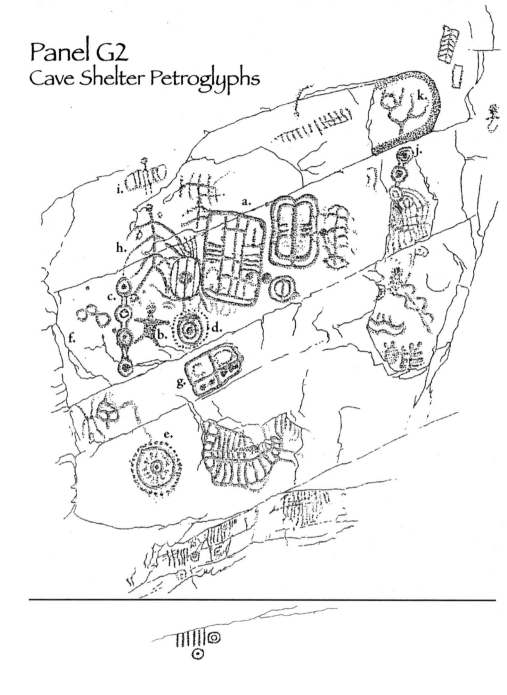

Fig. 12:3—Panel G2; bottom section located near a Middle Archaic fire pit

Numerous weathered petroglyphs were recorded in and adjacent to the cave shelter (A) in 6 panels, and in its small annex (B) shelter in 3 panels. The large G2 panel was composed around a large central box (a) sectioned with a variety of number combinations to possibly encode the full calendar system with a probable new year date. The many figures surrounding this mysterious box define its calendar relationships.

I interpret the man at the left center (b) with outstretched arms and legs as the shaman recording his astronomical observations on this panel and directing its inspection, so the narrative logically starts with him. His pointing arms and left leg tie two cross-quarter circles (c) in a 4 chain ($2 \times 45 = 90$) to a 3-concentric circle with 30 dots (d) for a 3-month quarter ($3 \times 30 = 90$). The same moon quarter below (e) with 15 full-moon spokes added has a trail line rising to a 3-part circle, apparently another 3-month quarter sign. The man's left arm also points across the 4-chain to 3-moon circles (f) for another quarter sign. His right leg points down to a quartered box (g) containing a crescent moon, sun, 2 dots and 3 dots, all tools for cross-quarter and quarter season observations.

Figures above the shaman and to the right move into the sky realm with spirit figures for recording the astronomical cycles. At the two sides are four concentric suns in vertical chains that frame the main panel (c and j). These 8 circles (4 on each side) are each a little different to distinguish its position in the 8 cross-quarter cycles in the year that makes up the four quarter seasons.

The left circles chain has an ascending motion above the shaman from the stick man (h) to a winged figure (i) at the top. The stick "spider" man (8 limbs) rises off the top sun on the chain, which should be ascent at summer solstice on this northern side. So, this side 4-circle chain pictures the four 45-day cross-quarter periods from winter solstice at the bottom to summer cross-quarter top circle (May 4 to June 21) for the summer growing season. The spider man's limbs on the other side come off a concentric sun oval divided into its four cross-quarter divisions with 6 lines off the top for the 6-month transit between the solstices.

On the right side, the motion in the right 4-circle chain (j) is reversed, descending from the summer cross-quarter at the top (June 21 to August 5). Bands falling down from the third circle highlight the autumn harvest and winter renewal seasons with a great flared design. A tree-like object above (k) with a circle in its branches is set inside a broadly pecked U recess that follows a natural crack line. The trunk rises above the circles chain. My impression is that this "tree" is actually a map of the Gap pass and eastern horizon ridges with the circle being the winter cross-quarter sun that rises in a notch against the north cliff (Fig. 12:2). This centers between the two cross-quarters at the bottom of the 4-circle chain where there is a sun circle in the plumage to celebrate completion of autumn harvest and the winter season of renewal. The plumage may also relate to bird migrations south during this time of year (cf. Panel D7).

The large middle box (a) is divided up like a calculator into a variety of sections and numbers that can be used with different combinations and multipliers to plot the various calendar cycles in the year. I have analyzed it in detail in the following Area H discussion of the Venus-Sun Conjunction. This box and the adjacent split box have deeply grooved lines. A stone tool that could have been used for the grooving was discovered during the excavation. The right box (l) is split down the middle with three lines inside each side, probably as 3-month quarter signs. This figure was modified from the mirrored, 4-quarter tree depicted in panels C12 and F7 which is shown by the connecting sides as not being deeply grooved. The tree at the side lays out the 6-month branches on each side for the full year. Directly above, the full year count is laid out again by a row of 12 lines separated by a long equinox line for the two 6-month halves of the year. A crescent "moon" above confirms these moon counts. The same year plot is in a double-comb box at the upper right corner with 6-month sections on either side.

Panel G7
Cave Polaris North Star Panel

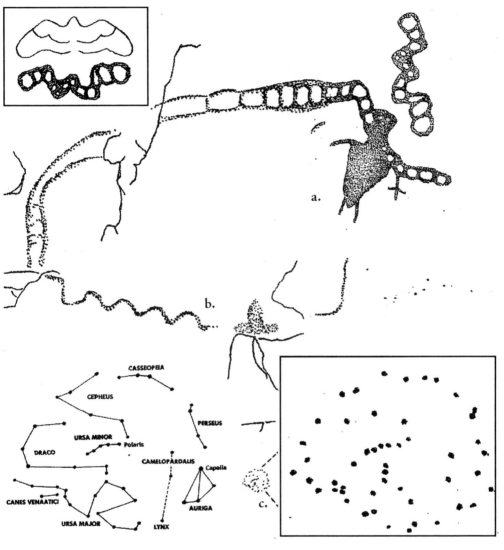

Fig. 12:4

Panel at upper left of Cave Entry. Panel faces Polaris on Narrows north peak. Stipple inset rubbing (actual size) with northern stellar horizon circle constellations interpretation. Inset at upper left compares calendar figure above god to an eagle in flight.

This panel is located on a sloping rock under an overhang to the upper left of the cave entrance. The absence of other petroglyphs on the adjacent cliff indicates the panel has a direct connection to the shelter. A large Fremont god (a) has a bird talon hand as a sign of his sky realm. He may be a link to the cave with the natural Tobats god-mask on the cliff above the panel. An eagle shaped year glyph flies above the god's head (see eagle drawing inset). It has four groups of 3 moons that match the 4 seasons. The eagle was highly revered as a sun symbol by Native Americans for its majestic bearing and its high flight seeming to communicate with the gods in the heavens.

On the god's right side is the familiar moon ladder with six circles (6 months), 3 extending off his arm with 3 fingers (2, 3-month seasons in a half year). The bird fingers recall Numic creation myths about the 3-month season originating from counting the bird's toes so winter would not be too long (Anne M. Smith, *Ute Tales*, 1992; and *Shoshone Tales*, 1993).

Another calendar chain or planetary band runs across the god's shoulder and head in a large arching path that circles into a wavy line across the bottom to a "seed" cone (b). The wave with 9 turns qualifies for the 9-month winter gestation cycle. The path line curves up beyond the cone to the god above to complete a circle.

There has to be an explanation for this panel being up high where it was difficult to reach and is hard to see on the sloping light rock. As I studied the panel's position, I discovered it aligns due east and faces due north to the Narrows north peak. When I put a square on the panel it pointed directly to the top of the north peak. On a hunch, I climbed onto a narrow ledge after dark so my head was next to the Fremont god, as if looking through his eyes. There, in a notch on top of the north peak, sat the North Star. This indescribable revelation was a master key to unlock the Parowan Fremont cosmology. The god's circular planetary band represents the stellar calendar rotation around the Polaris North Star. The night sky journey is labeled by a bold inverted U (not shown) at the bottom with a trail side coming off a stipple "star" (c) circle (compare Panel F11).

The final obscure figure is the most profound. Out of the blue, the idea struck me that a little 5 cm.-wide disc with 51 stipple dots is the northern stellar horizon circle rotating around the North Star. The photo inset is a rubbing for accuracy, and the constellation map is my interpretation (assisted by Joel Clements). While not perfect, the overall match is amazingly accurate for a free hand sketch. The position of the Big Dipper (Ursa Major), assuming an observation in the early night sky, dates this star map to early August coinciding with the August 12th 260-day Fremont New Year sun-dagger marker in the adjacent cave.

Quoting from *The Mythology of the Americas*, the "Big Dipper or Great Bear is one of the most striking constellations in the northern sky. Because the arrangement of stars is so clear, and it rises and sets in a predictable cycle through the year, it was an important marker of seasonal change among many northern people" (Jones and Malyneaux 2002: 25). The right angle seasonal positions of the Dipper through the year are, bottom-autumn, east-winter, top-spring, west-summer. Because the stars complete a full circle rotation in 24 hours, an early morning observation six hours later shifts the Dipper position counter-clockwise, 90 degrees on the North Star clock.

Master Astronomical Panels & Comparative Interpretations

Area H

Fig. 13—Area H Cliffs Map

Area H is located on east end of Narrows, south side, facing east.

Tracking a Venus-Sun-Moon Conjunction

Area H with its Master Panels on the high cliffs with a clear panoramic view of the eastern horizon, is where ancient astronomers probed deep space exploring harmony between the heavens and nature. Amazing sun-moon-Venus conjunction records detected here require deep analysis beneath petroglyph surfaces where the richest treasures of ancient knowledge are hidden.

The first Venus star cycle petroglyph was deciphered on Panel H1 and is also found on Panels H2, H3, J1, C5, G2 and A7 (see Fig. 14:1). The full study of these Venus petroglyphs is covered in this section. I wish to express appreciation to Astronomer Dr. John P. Pratt for checking the astronomical data in the analyses of the panels in this section.

Panel H1

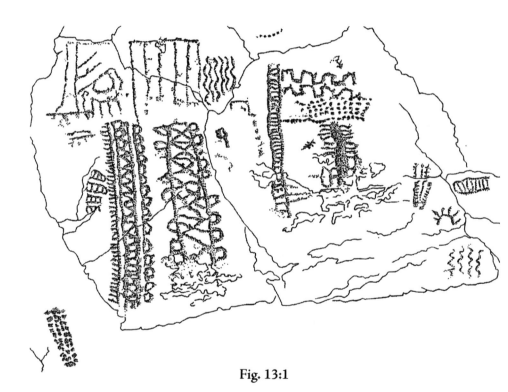

Fig. 13:1

This large panel facing east on a high ledge above the cave shelter is ideally suited as an eastern horizon observatory lookout. The cliff god face above the Polaris panel (G7) and cave is directly off the ledge so they doubtless relate to this panel. Here the planet and star rises could be viewed and plotted on the panel. A trail should eventually be made above the steep and hazardous talus slope to provide a closer look.

The ledge face where the priest-astronomer sat has a single petroglyph (H1b, no illustration) of a god with bird-talon hands and arms raised like wings. He rises over a planetary disk on a natural right (south) arc path over his head. Four adjacent foot prints suggest tracking the planets in their risings through the four seasonal quarters of the year, which had to be observed over many years to track Venus to its 2,920-day (8 year) solar conjunction recorded on the panel above. Parowan sky watchers recorded these events two hundred and fifty years before the Mayan astronomers recorded them in the Dresden Codex for an A.D. 934 Venus first appearance "heliacal" rise. Malm- strom (1997: 177–183) thinks the discovery could have originated in Central Mexico as recorded in the Codex Borgia, perhaps at Cholula, as the pilgrimage center of the creator life god Quetzalcoatl—the Toltec horned-bird-serpent and god of the Morn- ing Star depicted on the Gap Panel A10.

As I write, the morning paper announces NASA's latest spacecraft successfully entering orbit around Mars. Yesterday's paper pictured Saturn's moon Enceladus taken by the Cassini spacecraft with it's ice cap "raising the tantalizing possibility that the celestial object harbors life." Fascinating as this outer space journey is, there is an ironic neglect of knowledge of ancient Native American astronomical obser- vations accumulated over millennia that explored the creation of earth life through emergence and regeneration with the seasonal growing life-cycles moving in harmony with the heavens.

Panel H1a
Sun, Moon, and Venus Glyphs

Starting at the right of the cliff face, a crescent with 6 rays marks the 6 month solar transit. The 8-division ladder above indicates the 8 cross-quarters. Four rising snakes below have 6 turns that are observation tabulations.

At the left, two large vertical numeral glyphs up to 100 cm. (3 ½ ft.) long under a huge 6-comb dominate this panel record. The left one has a center band containing a wavy line with 30 turns for a lunation day count. A comb on the left side has 44 or 45 teeth for a cross-quarter. The right side has a row of 15 moons, a full moon count. This formal weaving panel recalls a Navajo tradition about the moon being the goddess of weaving. The wavy count design reflects the moon's weaving path that shifts each night, in addition to its two minimum and two maximum "warp" standstills in its 18.6-year Metonic cycle. The upper left crescent "moon" has 5 lines attached below and 3 diagonal lines above in a side comb. To the right side, a narrower vertical ladder panel and adjacent weathered figures like so many others appear to record moon cycles.

We next examine the proposed Venus weave panel.

Venus has similar maximum and minimum cycles as does the moon, and a much more unpredictable weaving pattern. This led me to suspect the adjacent vertical glyph with its erratic weave is an attempt to track the shifting Venus rises and moon rises along the eastern horizon. The Venus star rises in the east just before the sun during its Morning Star phase. Venus goes through three major phase shifts before returning as Morning Star after a short disapearance. The day numbers of the Venus Synodic Cycle, based on the Aztec record are:

243 +	Days of Morning Star visibility
77 +	Inferior Conjunction; dark phase days between Morning and Evening Star
252 +	Days of Evening Star visibility
12	Superior Conjunction; Invisible days return to Morning Star heliacal rise
584 =	Total days of the complete Venus Cycle

(Malmstrom 1997:217)

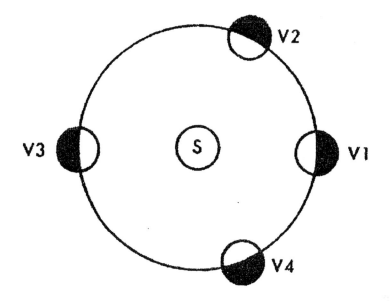

Fig. 13:3—Phases of Venus
(Moore 1968: 56)

Venus Cycle Compared to Aztec Record

	Aztec Days
V1. Inferior conjunction, about a week	12 days
V2. Morning Star, about 8 months; western morning elongation (mid point)	243 days
V3. Superior conjunction, about 10 weeks (behind sun)	77 days
V4. Evening Star, about 8 months; eastern elongation (mid point)	252 days
	584 days

Fig. 13:4

A large 6-comb for a half year hovers directly over the Venus glyph with its left tooth attached to a line count of 15 circles (half lunation) below at the side of the moon glyph.

The Venus glyph has 8 circles (solar transits) on each side to define its 8-year cycle.

Five Venus cross (X) glyphs down the middle weave represent 5 Venus cycles of 584 days each (5 × 548 = 2,920 days). Seeing the connections between the moon and Venus weaving panels, I suspected a possible moon cycle conjunction may be recorded. Of course that could not be known without extensive observations and record keeping during the period of the Venus Synodic Cycle.

I started with the two circles inside the Venus glyph between the 2 and 3 crosses. My guess is that these circles indicate watching the moon through two Venus cycles. Checking the moon against Venus, 19.77 moons × 29.53 moon days = 548 (Venus cycle). 19.77 rounds off to 20, so I looked for a record of 20. Off the left of the panel I found a block of 4 rows of dots that total 42. Three left dots are scratched so the total may be 39. How many moons are there in 2 Venus cycles? There are 39.54. This begins the search for a moon conjunction. The conjunction totals for Venus, sun and moon are:

Venus	584 × 5 = 2920 days
Sun	365 × 8 = 2920 days
Moon month	29.5 × 99 = 2920.5 days

The prominent lunar panel and its tie to the solar-Venus conjunction panel give the distinct impression that the sky shamen were looking for a lunar-solar-Venus conjunction. The 2,920-day sun-Venus conjunction does, in fact, come very close to 99 moons (99 × 29.5 = 2,920.5). A long lunar ladder to the right has 25 steps with a detached larger ladder below with 4 steps for a total of 29. Two wavy moon count paths extend right from the top of the ladder. This ties to a section of 5 rows of dot counts (5 shamen records?). The dot totals are 14 + 10 + 11 + 11 + 24 = 70. Added to the ladder, 70 + 29 = 99. These numbers are confirmed by a duplicate record on Panel H2.

Relative dating of this fantastic panel with its other Gap panel connections has to be assessed for considering extended cultural relations. I will propose a mind buster up front. Parowanites had been making astronomical observations for about 250 years before the first record of the Venus-solar conjunction of 2920 days was recorded in Mesoamerican codices. Citing Malmstrom (1997: 177–183), Floyd Lounsbury (1983) argued persuasively that the Maya "Venus table" in the Dresden Codex (written between A.D. 1200 and 1300) was historically set in motion on a Maya date equivalent to November 20, A.D. 934. On that morning, a heliacal (beginning) rising of Venus occurred which Lounsbury has called "a unique event in historical time," because it came exactly three Great Cycles after the base date of the Dresden Codex. Several meshing cycles are involved in this conjunction: 146 × 260 days = 65 × 584 days = 2 × 52 × 365 days = 37960 days (base date) = 104 years (two 52-year cycles).

It may be too great a stretch to propose that the earlier record at the Gap observatory could be the origin for the Mesoamerican Venus conjunction vision, transported along the Toltec turquoise trade route. Malmstrom (1997) focused on Cholula as a possible place of origin, because it was a major worship center of Quetzalcoatl who was resurrected as the Morning Star. We have recognized the large horned-bird-serpent god image on Panel A10, who was Quetzalcoatl among the Toltecs, as the central figure on A10 tied to the 260-day calendar and summer solstice. The god image is also central on the V–Gap Map petroglyph (A7). These had to be developed or were developing concepts early in the history of Parowanite astronomy in the 8th century A.D. when these major panels were created. We cannot imagine them being left blank through two or three hundred years of occupation history in the cave shelter. The master Maya astronomers, on the other hand, don't have the Venus conjunction cycle recorded until the 10th century A.D. (Malmstrom 1997: 183).

It is easier to recognize shared knowledge exchange rather than trying to pin down ultimate origins. With the Mesoamerican type village plan at Paragonah (see Parowan Gap Sacred Space Section), I can also imagine a few Mesoamerican settlers in the turquoise trade business influencing cultural exchange, including shared astronomical knowledge recorded at the Gap observatory. On the other hand, the depth of antiquity at the Gap observatory, going back 5,000 years in the cave shelter, must keep an open door for considering possible Archaic astronomy origins on a developmental level we have not considered before. Such as it is, there are a lot more questions to explore in this un-trod territory.

Panel H2

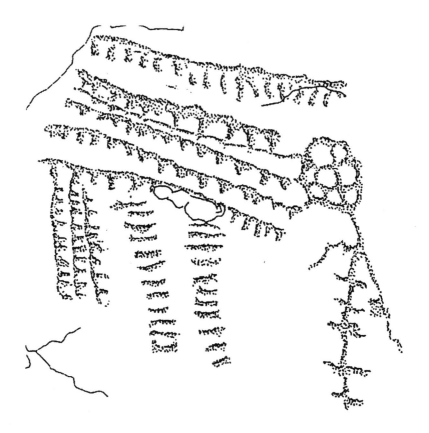

Fig. 13:5

A second lunar tabulation is located to the left. There are 5 horizontal combs like the 5 dot lines in H1. The numbers differ but the total is the same: 16 + 11 + 13 + 15 + 15 = 70. Three vertical combs attached match the H1 ladder total (11 + 10 + 9 = 29) for an 8-comb total of 99. That this is the 8-year Venus conjunction is confirmed by the sun flower "year" glyph with 8 sections. A double 6-comb below for the two halves of the year confirms the 8-year flower symbol above. Two columns of 11 and 12 lines are a different tabulation. I suspect these lines record 23 conjunction observations that were made over a 184 year period to track the lunar-solar-Venus conjunction. It might also involve an 8-year conjunction ritual celebration.

Panel H3a
Big Spiral

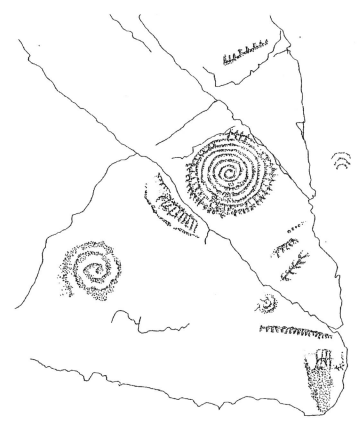

Fig. 13:6

This large panel is on a steep sloping rock. The right section centers on a large 7-turn spiral, the largest at the Gap (40 cm. wide), with numeral sun-ray tics around the outer 2 turns. Two sections are damaged. About 23 tics in two different quarters (doubled) project a 91–92-day quarter. Four prominent tic lines at the top end of the spiral could code 4 quarters for the year. The 7-turn spiral could be a division code for the year into seven 52-day cycles (7 × 52 = 364). These large spirals elsewhere are associated with the solstice. The 7-turn spiral could measure 7 months from winter solstice to August cross-quarter to begin the gestation fertility cycle highlighted in the cave. A curved comb on the left has 15 teeth along a curved line for a full moon tally, which faces a prominent 3-turn spiral for a 3-month quarter. A long comb at the lower right has 19 tics (lunar Metonic cycle?). Other figures are typical calendar counts.

Panel H3c
Venus–Solar Conjunction Observatory Record

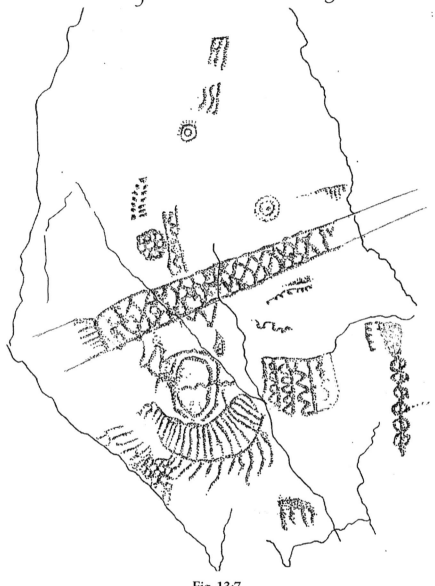

Fig. 13:7

The left section of Panel H3 is the largest cross weaving panel at the Gap, measuring a full 1.5 meters long. Relative figure size indicates importance, so this is a very important subject panel at the Gap. The only larger figure is the V–Gap map on Panel A7. Two sets of path lines project below the cross-weave panel's base to two large superimposed circles below. This suggests to me an eclipse or conjunction sign. The circle is cradled in a large crescent ladder (24 steps) with comb lines below (compare Panel H1) running off the right side. This big tabulation is supplemented by over a dozen other typical surrounding calendar numerals. Five are 8s and four are 5s, which should ring a familiar bell with Panel H1's Venus conjunction record, and hints that we are looking at another Venus-solar conjunction observatory record.

The first indication for Venus is the similar cross panel with circles in the middle. There are 5 crosses at the left of the circles with another 8 crosses on the right which expands this panel record to 13 Venus years compared to 5 on the H1 panel with circles in the middle. The vertical line on the right apparently cuts the record off at 13 to encode the magic 8 conjunction number, even though these are Venus signs. The real solar 8 number rises above the end of the left 5th cross in an 8-turn serpent panel. A solar wheel on its side has 8 sections with a 9th "dark" pecked section at the base over a small crescent which I believe pictures heliacal rise of Venus and passage through about 8 lunations as Morning Star ($8 \times 30 = 240$) before disappearance again.

We don't see the clean lunation panel record here as on H1, which is not needed, but a different emphasis on tracking the solar conjunction. We can only guess about the number of Venus cycle observation years in this record. The 13 cross totals seem static, but a 7-comb weathered by rain runoff over the panels left end, and 4 dots above the panel, may be multipliers expanding the 13 Venus record over a considerable length of time. Most authorities agree that it would have taken many centuries of observations to identify and perfect an accurate day-count Venus-solar conjunction. We know $7 \times 13 = 91$ is a good quarter-year match, which translates to 104 Venus cycles. Another 4 dots multiplier would equal 416 cycles for 242,944 days or 665 years. If this is valid, and we can only guess, the Parowanites brought their Venus record to continue looking when they arrived and settled in Parowan Valley in the latter part of the 7th century A.D.

Are the superimposed circles below an eclipse or conjunction sign? The numbers should tell the story. Again, the main number codes identified in Panel H1 to look for are the 5 Venus years conjunction with 8 solar years. This means if we pick a Venus calendar event like heliacal rise (first appearance as Morning Star), or its last visibility as Morning Star before disappearance in 243 days, or first appearance as Evening Star in 320 days, it will take exactly 8 solar years (2,930 days) for the Venus cycle event to return to the exact same solar conjunction position. Let's look at the numbers.

Path lines extend down the left section of H3c and appear to weave across the two superimposed eclipse circles or conjunction signs. Other path lines extend down from the center section from the 5 and 8 crosses like "legs" and form a cross path below to the outer ring. A compressed circle on the right leg at the contact point suggests the limited visible light at Venus' approaching conjunction. If this is the Venus conjunction "eclipse" sign, then the attached numbers should tell the story. The target numbers to look for based on the Aztec record are in the Venus tables on the following page.

Aztec Venus cycle day counts

243		Morning Star visibility
+		
77		Dark phase between Morning and Evening Star
320	=	Morning Star to Evening Star (first appearances)
+		
264		Evening Star to Morning Star (first appearances)
584	=	Total days of the complete Venus Cycle

Astronomical cycle day count (Malmstrom 1997: 217)

244		Days of Morning Star visibility
+		
77		Invisible days between Morning and Evening Star
+		
252		Days as Evening Star
+		
12		Invisible days before return to Morning Star heliacal rise
584	=	Total days of the complete Venus Cycle

There is a clear crescent ladder record of 24 steps with a 5 turn serpent at its right tapered end: 5 × 24 = 120 × 2 = 240. Since half cycle records are typical at the Gap, we have a good prospect for the Morning Star phase as the conjunction record here. The attached comb is somewhat less than the ladder. A large cluster of circles in the middle of the comb, possibly 15 or 16 for a half moon count, has 5 comb teeth on the left and 11 on the right for 16 as a possible match count. If we add this to the 24 ladder the total is 40. Taking the next 8-turn serpent at the upper right as a multiplier, 8 × 40 = 320, which is the Morning Star to Evening Star phase day count. Since there is only about a 20 day difference between the Evening Star phase to Morning Star and its phase length, this difference could be coded as well, but is not apparent and may not have been an important overlapping number.

The few days of disappearance between the end of Evening Star and Morning Star ranged from only 8 to 12 days in various Native American observations. It is equally hard to tie down without other records, but either of the other serpent panel numbers at the right side with 9 and 7 turns could do the job. More tempting is the 8-turn serpent rising off the Venus panel at the end of the 5th cross, where the heliacal Morning Star wheel kicks in (observed above).

I would anticipate seeing a clear record for the 77-day "dark" phase between Morning and Evening Stars. Maybe this is where the 15 or 16 count in the comb or its circle cluster comes into play with the 5 multiplier ($5 \times 15 = 75$; $5 \times 16 = 80$).

Whatever the case may be in the final analysis, there is sufficient consistency in these observatory signs and numbers to conclude that we are indeed viewing a remarkably consistent observatory record for the Venus phases that were being tracked for solar conjunctions.

A final note. The two prominent figures at the lower right, like those at the lower right of Panel A7 can now be seen as a road sign announcing the trail of this panel record with a bold 4-comb for tracking the 4 seasons, and a chain of 6 moons (solar transit) with 5 dots off the side and a foot print off the top with a 5-comb on its side for tracking the Venus conjunction. The message seems clear. It is not impossible that the Venus heliacal rise conjunction date recorded in the Maya Dresden Codex, which is " 9.9.9.16.0, 1 Ahuau, 18 Kayab = February 6, A.D. 623" (Malmstrom 1999: 181), is recorded on this panel which has marked the 5-dot year Venus-Solar conjunction on the 3rd circle from the bottom. (This date is very close to the beginning of Fremont occupation in the Parowan Valley.) Based on the cross-quarter seasons, this is in the start or end month of the 3-month winter season centered on winter solstice, so the date is in the start or end of the 3rd quarter, putting the 3rd circle start by the 5 dots at the November 5 or February 5 cross-quarter to match the Dresden Codex record!

Since the Dresden Codex (written between A.D. 1200 and 1300) is looking back several centuries in time and is the only Maya record known of the Venus-solar conjunction, who is to say that their knowledge of this event did not come from Parowan? (Wauchope and Willey 1965: 637) The evidences grow, as observed in the H1 discussion, that the Toltecs and certainly the Aztecs shared this Venus knowledge exchange that may have started during the turquoise trade network passing through the Parowan Gap and Parowan Valley centuries before the Mesoamerican records appeared.

Panels H3d and H4b
260-Day Calendar Record

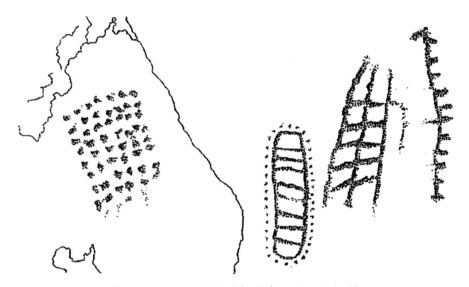

Fig. 13:7—Panel H3d (right) and H4b (left)

Panel H4b is a block of dots up slope from H3 on a bedrock boulder to the left of H4a overhang petroglyphs. Section 4a has a block of dots in 8 horizontal lines. The top 4 rows of dots have 7 each for 28, and the bottom 4 rows have 6 each for 24, which totals 52. (Two odd dots were later added to the right side out of line, and 5 or 6 irregular smaller dots were also added to the bottom.) This 52-day count almost certainly relates to a 40-day count on the adjacent Panel H3d as the two numbers that locate the 260-day cycle dates from August 12 to April 29 recorded on the V–Gap calendar Panel A7. These are the day counts from summer solstice and equinox that pinpoint these two dates on that panel. The 40 count with a 9-month glyph next to this 52 count on Panel H3d represents the gestation cycle meaning of the 260 days.

These two panel numbers were evidently placed on the highest southern rocks directly across the Narrows from Panel A7 to highlight their importance in the calendar. They are also the most distant southward numbers at the Narrows, which I think relates to the southern passage of the sun from August 12 to winter solstice and back to the matching observatory date on April 29 for this cycle. This record was probably made by calendar priests working from the nearby Panel H1 ledge. This may have even been the first observatory calendar plot at the Gap when the 260-day almanac was implemented, preliminary to constructing the sunset observatory cairns for these dates.

Venus–Sun–Moon Conjunctions

Decipherment of the three Venus conjunction panels in Area H provides the data necessary for recognizing Venus records on five other panels: J1, C5, G2, A10 and A7 that will be discussed in that order. A composite of these petroglyphs is in the figure below. First, an inventory of the basic conjunction signs identified in area H include:

- ✦ Double circle (eclipse-conjunction pictograph)
- ✦ Split circle (conjunction path line)
- ✦ Long 6-comb (6-month solar transit)
- ✦ Eight-year notation (sun conjunction period)
- ✦ Five crosses or circles (Venus conjunction period)

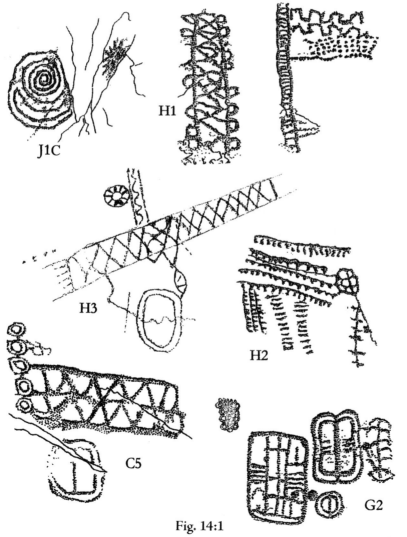

Fig. 14:1

Panel J1c
Venus Morning Star Observatory Station

Fig. 14:2

Given the level of astronomical knowledge recorded at the Parowan Gap, it should not be surprising to find a Venus observatory station. There may have been a preference for observing the pre-dawn Venus through its 243-day Morning Star rise phase at the east end of the Parowan Gap by Little Salt Lake. This location gives a clear view across the lake and valley. A section of rock outcrop facing east at the Area J site has a star burst with 8 light spires rising from a "horizon" crack as it appears on the horizon. A large adjacent spiral (40 cm. high) has 5 lunation turns then go into 3 wide half circle pendulum swings that turn back into the spiral for a total of 8. Based on the Area H Venus interpretations this figure qualifies for a Venus-sun conjunction—5 Venus cycles in 8 years.

I once recorded a similar petroglyph facing east along the Fremont River at Capitol Reef.

Panel C5
Venus Evening Star Observatory Station

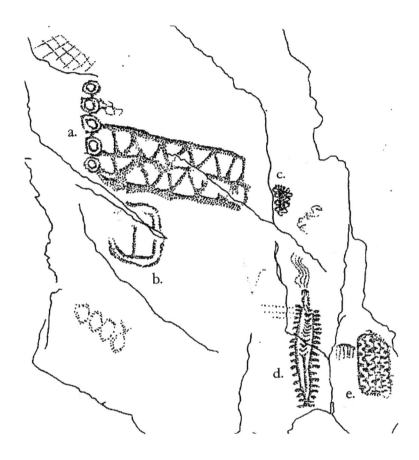

Fig. 14:3

This panel is below a ledge facing west on a high rock directly below the Narrows north peak (see Fig. 5 Area Map). It is ideally situated for a sun-moon-Venus set observation station. The main figure at the top (a.) is a double triangle panel with 4 triangles in each (8 total) and a chain of 5 double circles up the left side. The lower triangles were arranged to form a cross with the top center triangles (highlighted). A large double split circle is directly under the left triangles (b.). A foot print off the panel's right side (c.) has 5 toes and 8 circles on the sides (one on base). The total parallels with Area H figures are obvious for the 5–8 Venus-sun conjunction. We can anticipate finding cycle tallies in the various tabulations below.

One that stands out is a box of four wavy lines with 11 turns each (e) (weathered right side reconstructed), and a 6-comb attached to the side as a multiplier

(4 × 11 = 44 × 6 = 264). What can we make of this number? It is the Aztec day count for Venus as Evening Star through inferior conjunction to heliacal rise (see Area H introduction).

Is there also a 99 lunation conjunction count? An adjacent elongated U (d) has a trail ascending inside with 12 or 13 U-moon's and a fire on top with smoke ascending toward the Venus-sun conjunction foot above. Eighteen tics on the U's left and 19 on the right total 37. Added to the 12 or 13 U's the total is 49 or 50. If we multiply the foot-toes and circles and then add them: 5 × 9 = 45 + 50 = 95. This is 4 short of 99. The 4 connecting smoke lines complete the 99 count.

Panel G2
Venus-Sun Conjunction Boxes

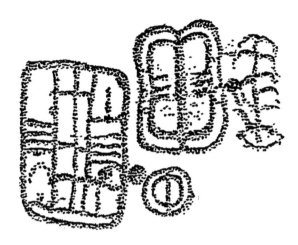

Fig. 14:4

The meaning of the large central boxes in the Cave Shelter Panel G2 became clear when I was correlating the other great conjunction cycle records. The main box has 5 vertical sections. The left one has 4 lines over a moon crescent above a dot which pictures a conjunction with the 4 quarters extending across the base. The two middle columns have 4 sections each for 8. The center compartment in the right section has 5 sections with the circle that ties to another circle outside the box that ties to the conjunction circle, which in turn labels the box. The top and bottom sections add 3 for an 8 total. This is the code for the 5–8 conjunction. Thus, we have cycles of 5 (Venus), 8 (sun) and moon seasons (year) all contained in one big conjunction box. The split circle matches the big circle above which incorporates the 4, 3-month quarter seasons of the year that measures the conjunction cycles. The tree on the right seems to tie the numbers together as a tree-of-life symbol; 5 branches on the right and 3 on the left total 8 with a conjunction sun circle at left center connected on a pathline to opposing crescents (moon and Venus?) at the base of the tree trunk.

Panel A10

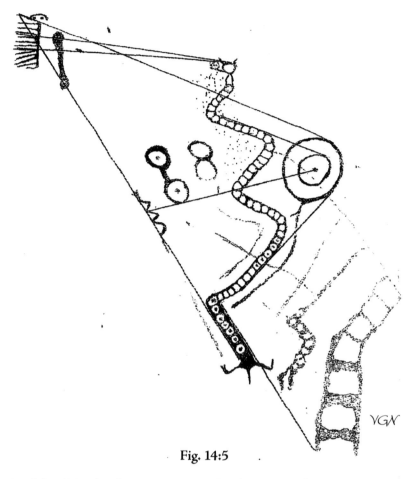

Fig. 14:5

Analysis of detail in the drawing warranted redrawing with greater precision. The principal creator rain-life god of the Aztecs was Quetzalcoatl (raised up or bird serpent). His image among the earlier Toltecs at Chichen Itza (Yucatan) was a horned, feathered serpent. These are the elements of the great six foot long serpent on Panel A10 (horns on head and bird legs on tail). This principal god of the Toltecs can be traced back a thousand years earlier. Rain dash lines fall from the A10 serpent's head as the bringer of the spring rains. Quetzalcoatl was also the creator of the calendar. The A10 serpent body is composed to portray the calendar cycles in day-count circles on six body sections (6-month solar transit), centered on a 4-quarter concentric sun that interacts with a summer solstice sunset shadow marker. The top five turns have a 45-day cross-quarter count (summer cross-quarter to summer solstice). The 52 total is the day count from April 29 New Year to June 21 summer solstice of the 260–105-day calendar. The bold tail with 7 concentric circles is a base calendar plot number $(7 \times 52 = 364)$ that originates from a lunar quarter.

The Hopi Snake Dance relates how the serpent represents the power to call up the creative life force for both man and nature. As the serpent power is taken up into the sky, the rain comes down. The last strike of a serpent in the ceremony brings the first stroke of lightning which releases the spring rain and initiates another growing season (Waters 1970: 321–24).

Panel A7
Venus-Sun-Moon Conjunction Dating

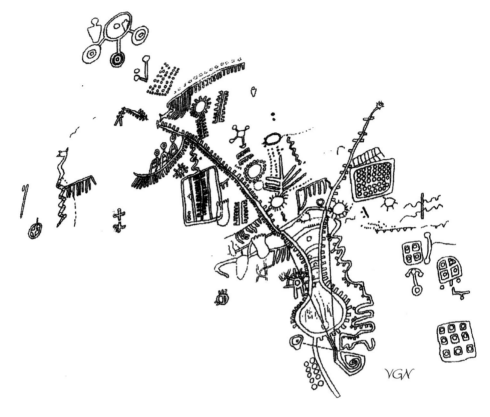

Fig. 14:6

A Venus serpent on the left of Panel A7 (above), related to the serpent on Panel A10, has 8 circled turns (conjunction years?). The serpent's tail points off to the right from a circled cross, which is a Venus glyph in Mesoamerica. (Fig. 14:7). Three dots above the cross may indicate the other three phases after Morning Star, as with the Venus spiral petroglyph (Panel J1c). A 9-month comb is attached to the serpent for the 260-day gestation cycle. The end tooth angles out to point down to two crosses (compare Panel A10). These are two Venus crosses (analyzed in Panel H1), which I believe here represent Morning Star and Evening Star. The Maya "Yax" glyph for Venus is two circles (dots or eyes) inside an inverted U, which is pictured next the pointing comb tooth on Panel A10 (Fig. 14:5). The Venus god in Sheep Wash (end of section) is the most graphic pictograph for this glyph.

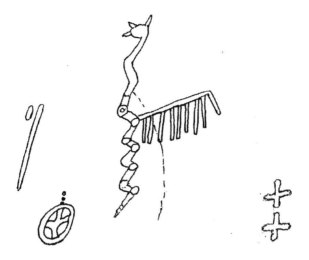

Fig. 14:7—Venus Serpent

Alternative numbers may encode the 243-day Morning Star phase. The cross points right to a lunation box with a 30-day comb ladder next to the V–Gap left arm (Fig. 14:6) through an 8-turn serpent (8 × 30 = 240). This count may be duplicated on the right arm with 40 tic days, also in the attached box, for a day count from Vernal equinox (March 21) to April 29–30 to complete the 260-day cycle. A large 6-comb attached to this arm could multiply the adjacent box for another Venus code—6 × 40 = 240.

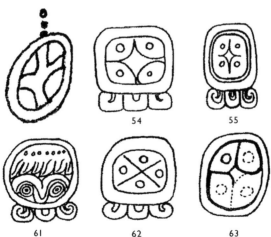

Fig. 14:8—Venus Glyphs
Parowan Gap Venus Glyph, Panel A7 (top left);
Mesoamerican Glyphs (54, 55, 61, 62, and 63)
in Mayan Hieroglyphics (Thompson 1960)

Venus Glyphs—Panel A7 (Right side) Figs. 14:6 and 14:9

Pictured below are three prominent dot boxes with adjacent signs that flow down from the 41-dot box off the V–Gap's right arm (Fig. 14:6). This section stands alone as a unit to highlight the 584-day Venus synodic cycle. These boxes ingeniously interlock with sun and moon cycle counts. The full 4-seasons year is symbolized in two 4-quarter boxes. The lower one has an equinox line between solstice dots with an arm marking a date dot off equinox (41-day box date above?). The 9-moon box below represents the 260-day cycle (9 moon months). The other 4 quarter year box has a Venus barbell (Morning Star/Evening Star) cycle glyph on its side and a Venus-solar conjunction glyph below, as I interpret.

How does this all tie to the 41-day box above? A full-moon day-count ladder in the 41-day box is a reduction sign. Similarly, a 5-ray sun falls off the lower right corner (compare 13-ray sunset on left) carrying the 41-day box reduction sign down toward the three boxes below. This can be interpreted as extracting the 41-day box from the 260 and 365 box totals: 365-41 + 260 = 584 days which is the Venus synodic cycle (see Area H discussions).

Fig. 14:9

Sun-Moon-Venus Conjunction Plots

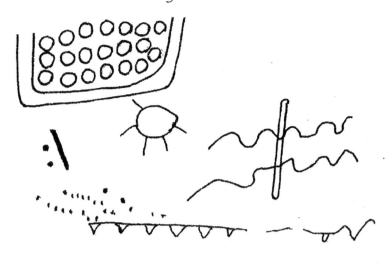

Fig. 14:10

Several sketchy number figures below the 41-day box for observatory plots reveal significant calculation notations for sun-moon-Venus conjunctions recorded in the adjacent big boxes. A group of 20 dots in three lines directly under the 41-day box extend off a 6-tooth comb. They are grouped like observations of three different moon watchers. They also slant to match the 5-moon circle overhead. The lower half of the upper box also has a 20 count set apart from the top formal 21 half, reinforcing the 20 dots moon count with the 5-moon. As a multiplier, this would equal 100 moons. What about a day count? $20 \times 29.53 = 590$; subtracting the attached 6-comb at the base, the sum is a 584 day count = the Venus cycle!

Could there be a Venus-lunar conjunction record here? If 100 moons were observed and noted during the Venus cycle observations, the sky watchers could have discovered a near 99 moons conjunction with the Venus-sun conjunction recorded on Panels H2 and H3. The day difference can be counted on one hand.

Moon	99×29.53	= 2923 days
Venus	5×584	= 2920 days
Sun	8×365	= 2920 days

Where is the sun-Venus junction record here? A vertical bar connects two wavy count lines. The top line has 8 turns. The bottom line has 6 turns, that could be 5 expanding turns to the left (Venus longer cycle) stretched out to match the 8 suns length. Their stretched out lengths are, in fact, equal. This apparent Venus-sun conjunction record explains the middle bar pointing down to the middle of the Venus glyphs group below.

So, here indeed is an abbreviated notation record for the prominent sun-moon-Venus cycles glyphs. The Parowan Fremont dedication to finding harmonic planetary conjunctions was perhaps not unlike ancient Mayan astronomers, driven by a belief that appropriate timely rituals for divine favors was possible from the celestial powers that controlled the cosmos (Aveni 1997: 182–186).

Venus Date

Vincent Malmstrom (1997) has provided some valuable Venus cycle tables from two ancient Mesoamerican books, the Mexican Codex Borgia and the Maya Dresden Codex. He plotted the Venus superior conjunction (last visible as Morning Star) and inferior conjunction (first Morning Star heliacal rise appearance from the Codex tables) as they would appear in 1992 and 1993 respectively. I was startled when I came upon his dates to see that they coincide with the three dates I had previously deciphered on the V–Gap calendar map.

The right arm of the V–Gap map record (Fig. 14:11) is split at the center point by the horizon line sunset on April 29 (260-day completion date) and May 5 (cross-quarter) sunset. There are obviously dates above and below where the sun sets, with 15 or 16 days above and 24 below.

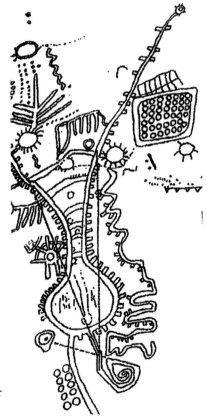

There are 40 day tics on this right arm plus 1 day adjuster at the base. Forty records the days from March 21 equinox to April 29. A 6-comb adds 6 days to May 5. The large 40–41 dot box confirms the arm numbers. The corresponding horizon observatory date on April 29–30 ends the 260-day cycle and year at superior conjunction on the same date recorded in the Dresden Codex.

Now, what is the arm's top 16-day date? It is simply a straight day count from the March 21 equinox to April 6. In basic astronomy, this could be a full moon from a new moon at equinox. There is, in fact, an inverted last phase moon crescent at the left center of this upper right arm. But something more is going on. A double 8-comb for 16 at the right is rising from or descending into the 41 box. This could be the moon, but possibly a moon conjunction as well. Malmstrom (1997: 179–180) identifies the inferior conjunction of Venus, which is its first brief appearance and disappearance just before dawn (heliacal rise as Morning Star), as occurring on

Fig. 14:11

April 5 in the Dresden Codex, and April 7 in the Codex Borgia. Before these dates came to my attention, I had analyzed the box and right section figures below as recording the Venus-sun conjunction (see preceding discussion). We can now conclude that the main target date for marking that conjunction was April 6, the heliacal rise of Venus (a day variance occurs some years due to the odd day in the year requiring a leap year adjustment.) Due to Venus' 584-day synodic period, the next heliacal rise from April 6 will be 584 days later on November 11 the next year. Based on the 5/8 Venus-sun synodic conjunction record at the Gap, Parowan priests understood that a fixed Venus date would return to the same solar date in 8 years. So the April 6, 1993 date returned in 2001 and will return again in 2009, 2017, etc.

Technically, Venus will slip backward from a given date 2.34 days, which means the exact same date will occur every 1249 years in our calendar for an April 5–7 heliacal rise. These fixed dates in two Mesoamerican codices and in the V–Gap calendar reveal the date was probably an actual event that became fixed in these records by tradition for ongoing ritual commemoration. We can use Aveni's (1980: 84–85) figures for precision calculation in the 8-year conjunction cycles (99 moons = 2923.53; 8 suns = 2,921.94; 5 Venus = 2919.6). We can calculate the year when this date occurred on April 6 as A.D. 744, which is tempting for the period when these records originated. Earlier dates that fall with the Gap Archaic history are B.C. 505, 1754, and 3003.

It would certainly be a huge plus if an April 6 observatory cairn, designated XC-1, existed to confirm this date. The location was found with additional field work in 2005, but is not recorded in this study for its protection until the preservation enhancement program at the Gap is in place.

Our final search for the Venus-sun conjunction record has to be conducted on the V–Gap calendar map (see Fig. 14:6).

The 260–105-day divisions of the year account for the imbalance in the left and right arms of the V–Gap map, and also accommodates a 548-day Venus synodic cycle count, as we shall see. Following the half cycles structure on the V–Gap calendar, we count down the right arm, out and back on the inner 6-comb, and down to the lobe base for 52 (+1) days, half of the 105-day summer season. The 130 remaining days in a half year on the left arm (52 + 130 = 182), doubles for the 260-day, 9 month winter gestation season (130 × 2 = 260). This structure confirms the 260–105-day cycles as the major divisions for the solar year on the V–Gap calendar map.

The ultimate origin of the 260-day cycle has remained a mystery in Mesoamerica, but may now be revealed at the Parowan Gap as originating from Venus. Final confirmation in this decipherment would be a 260-day calendar count on the left arm for Venus' Evening Star phase to the April 6 heliacal rise on the horizon point, which would also confirm the 260-day calendar count from August 12 to April 29 recorded at the V–Gap horizon line, which would in turn link to the Venus cycle. Checking the numbers, both arms and smaller comb tic counts total 182 (plus 1 at the base) for a half year. We remove the 15 tics on the upper right arm (above the horizon line) to look for the 260 count (183 − 15 = 168). 168 subtracted from 260 leaves a 92-day quarter balance needed (260 − 168 = 92). The two long (horizontal) 23-count combs next to the upper left arm now come forward with fanfare. Doubled (counted out and back) they present two full 46-day cross-quarters totaling 92-day quarter year count.

Finally, the 584-day Venus synodic cycle almost certainly has to be coded on the V–Gap map (Panel A7, Fig. 14:6, Figs. 6:5–8). Since it exceeds the year count, it has to involve the large attached arms. If we add the 260 cycle count identified above to the 365-day year, the total is 625, just 41 too long. This number immediately rings a bell with the right arm 41 count. So the 584 Venus days end on the return count at the blank section on the bottom of the V–lobe at the left of the right arm's 41 days. This blank space must be the 8-day disappearance of Venus at its inferior conjunction. Note how its length matches the section with 8 tics (above left). To confirm this, there has to be a Venus observatory sign tied to the blank section for inferior conjunction and heliacal rise. A lobed concentric sun circle (Venus-sun conjunction sign?) stands at the left side of the observatory trail sign tied to summer solstice (Cairn A3), where a Venus observation station was tracked to the south (left) for viewing Venus' northern standstill in the Narrows (projected on the horizon map. That interpretation is now confirmed by the spiral observatory path pointing to the concentric lobe. The spiral point tip in turn ties to a pointer on the terrain map aligned to the trail head by the 16 date at the horizon sunset where the inferior conjunction sunset date is followed by heliacal rise, 16 days after March 21 equinox on April 6 (discussed above). Fixed cycles, not fixed dates, were the prime concern in ancient calendars.

The heliacal rise of Venus was celebrated every 8 years at the Gap with a lunar-solar conjunction. This is not to say that superior conjunction and appearance as Evening Star were not observed for conjunction as well, only that heliacal rise was most important. This event was also fixed on the V–Gap calendar 16 days after Vernal equinox for possible annual commemoration, since that sunset date in the Narrows is also fixed by the Cairn XC–1 observatory station I discovered in 2005.

We have crossed all the bridges to confirm the Venus-sun conjunction record based on the 260-day Venus Evening Star cycle anchored to the 260-day fixed segment of the year between August 12 and April 29 which was probably set on April 6, A.D. 744. This prevailed throughout ancient Mesoamerican calendars.

Malmstrom (1997) made a compelling argument for the 260-day cycle's origin at Izapa, Mexico, based on the 260-day southern zenith passage of the sun at Izapa's 15 degree north latitude. The Parowan Gap now presents a more compelling case for a Venus origin, meaning that the Izapa temple center must have been located where the sun's zenith passage would celebrate the Venus cycle. In January 1998, I conducted a theodolite survey of the Tajumulco peak at Izapa, Mexico and found Venus' northern maximum standstill rises directly over the pointed peak. So that site had to be originally located no later than 400 B.C. where it could commemorate that event with a Venus alignment to the Mt. Tajumulco mountain peak.

The heliacal rise of Venus on April 6 at Parowan Gap in A.D. 744 would have occurred at Izapa, Mexico in 505 B.C. as the possible anchor date. My prior work at Izapa identified a heliacal rise of Venus recorded on Stela 50 (Norman 1976), which is aligned with a pillar-ball "Venus star" monument to the Tajumulco "Venus" peak (Norman 1980). The pillar is set in front of Stela 10 that records completion of the 260-day cycle with its split cartouche glyph in the sky panel. The monument also records the event in its calendar month in May as a fixed segment of the year. The pillar-ball also aligns with two other pillar-ball monuments on the horizon rise and set azimuths for zenith passage to mark the 260-day cycle (Norman, Izapa Calendar 1976).

Finally, the Venus record at the Gap is complemented by a wonderful Venus humanoid god I discovered on a remote petroglyph panel on the Green River in the Uintah Basin in 1979. A star burst like the Gap star (Panel J) is held up in the god's hand. His other hand is an east-west pointer for his pointing eyes that are set apart on the ends of a U-head to represent the Morning Star and Evening Star phases of Venus. The head is under a dotted starry sky band for these two phases of Venus. Long wavy path lines to the side (not shown) indicate Venus's wandering path through the sky.

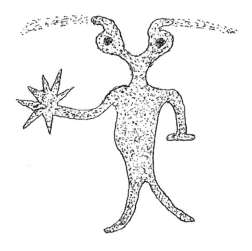

Fig. 14:12—Venus humanoid god from Uintah Basin

Parowan Gap
Sacred Space

There are Certain Mountains
Indians know are Holy Places

You can tell which ones they are
Because storm clouds gather at their peaks
And lightning strikes more often
Than it does on other mountains
And eagles circle in the afternoons
And winds begin up there.

Those are the mountains
Where the power of ancient spirits
Still hover like a mist.
Those are the mountains
Where gods still live and plant their corn
And dance.

In the southwest, each tribe has a homeland
Marked off by sacred mountains
And each mountain has a story . . .

Byrd Baylor, *The Way to Make Perfect Mountains—*
Native American Legends of Sacred Mountains (1997: 4)

Reprinted with permission from Cinco Puntos Press. From "The Way to Make Perfect
Mountains" by Byrd Baylor (1979), Cinco Puntos Press. www.cincopuntos.com

The vision of the Gap as a massive calendar observatory is a function less known in
ancient Mesoamerican temple centers. My astronomy work at Izapa, Mexico, which
prepared me for the Gap Project, is probably the most developed Mesoamerican calendar temple center. It may predate the Parowan Fremont by about a thousand years.

I have come to expect astronomical orientations in architecture. A Paragonah
plaza alignment to winter solstice sunrise, and the villages of Paragonah, Parowan, and
Summit (Middian Village) lined up toward winter solstice sunset reflect a widespread

and ancient community design plan that brought a sense of cosmic harmony and order to community life. Temple centers were the optimum in this kind of design planning. The Parowan Gap as a sacred center might have gone farther in the direction of cosmic temple design planning if architecture had been introduced. Or would it? There is much more beyond our observatory cairns and petroglyphs at the Parowan Gap that opens into a massive natural wilderness temple center which includes the entire three mile stretch through the Parowan Gap and beyond. It stretches a mile west to the most distant observatory station shrine. It stretches in a straight sight line east another five miles across Parowan Valley to Parowan Village, perhaps coincidently for there are no visible remains in Parowan today on which to focus. If valid, the total distance is about nine miles.

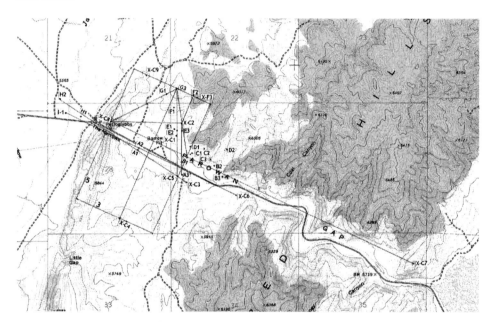

Fig. 15:1—Four peaks Sacred Space by 3 × 5 Rectangle (Norman 2002)

Results of ARCON's Gap Project focused initially on the immediate Gap Narrows petroglyph, cave, and camp sites with a few projected observatory cairns. By the end of the Project 33 cairns were catalogued. About half were identified within or near other prehistoric sites. Many rock cairns that do not have direct artifact associations or solar alignments have proven to be ancient survey markers. Some lay out sacred space.

Cairns were placed strategically on tops of hills at right angles on the four sides of the east Gap basin. These cairns form a 3 × 5 rectangle. The central right angle axis of the hill cairns extends three miles east on a 115° axis to the hilltop cairn by the Little Salt Lake at the east entrance to the Gap. This happens to square at 25° with the west mountain ridge line at the Gap Narrows. The west Gap mountain Cairn X–C8 was located down slope at a point where it aligns across the basin to the east hill observatory Cairn B1 on a straight line two miles on through the Gap to the east hilltop cairn (X–C7) by Little Salt Lake. Cairn X–C4 on the south basin peak was located down the ridge from the top toward the east to a point where it aligned with the north peak cairn G3 at a right angle to the pass-line cairns. This also formed a 3 × 5 rectangle or projected rectangle encompassing the basin. This rectangle and hills represents the four quarters based on a "golden mandala" geometric code that is an ancient expression of sacred space. This dimension is also found in the architecture and design of a Fremont house at Paragonah.

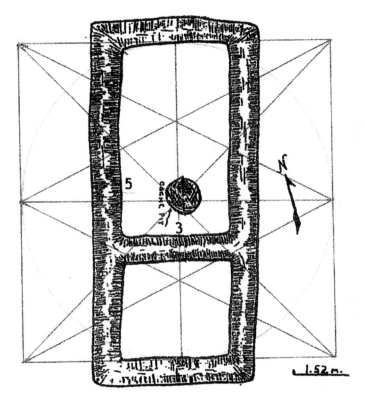

Fig. 15:2—Paragonah Fremont Village House
(Meighan, et al. 1956; geometry analysis added by G. Norman)

The Tewa site planning in New Mexico is perhaps the closest known system of marking the boundaries of Tewa sacred space with simple rock cairn shrines that can be compared to the Gap (Ortiz 1973: 18–19). Southwest recognition of the system and the four quarters world view to four sacred mountains is well established. Architecture orientations to the sun, moon, and Venus cycles are well known. These are sophisticated trademarks of high civilization. We certainly would not expect this in the Fremont world with a limited population.

Early settlers in Parowan Valley reported about 400 mounds associated with the four villages, which would have sustained a population of between about 2,000 and 2,500 people. The Parowan Fremont was clearly on the rise to a distinctive and sophisticated civilization. Another unique feature of the cairns layout was a north-south sight line from Cairn X–C5. It is positioned ¾ mile on a NS sight line with Cairn G3 on top of the basin's north peak, fixed to Polaris with a plumb bob. Both of these cairns were vandalized by apparent treasure hunters, unaware that these surface cairns are not burial markers. Some rocks and rock holes, plus site record maps and photos

Fig. 15:3—Rock Geo-form Map of Gap Pass
Some stones were slightly rearranged temporarily for
this photo to visualize the terrain comparison.

made restoration possible. The Polaris line is also close to Cairn E2 near the equinox Cairn E1. This was a special revelation of the site plan for it brought the Polaris cosmic center of the universe into the Gap micro-cosmic temple center with equinox symbolizing the earthly center transect and the Polaris North Star the cosmic navel of the earth.

After recording the east hill cairn X–C7, I was impressed that this was no ordinary cairn, but a Geo-form of some kind. The rock's position on the hard, narrow rocky ridge must be pretty much in the same place where they were laid perhaps a thousand years ago, except for a little dislocation by animals stepping on them. The variety is curious: large and small cobblestones and a couple of sandstone slabs, in a general U shape facing west. They seem to be a stone "map" of the Gap pass terrain. The eight rocks were selected to match the eight visible ridge formations that cross and flank the pass along the three mile stretch to the west Narrows ridge. The long loaf shaped cobble stone on the left is a very good visual for the Narrows south mountain. The large sandstone slab on the right is also a good match for the high Red cliffs that command the north side view. A little cobble stone matches the north peak of the Narrows, barely visible behind another long cobblestone ridge. Initially there was no rhyme or reason for this Geo-form. Only after I discovered the long central axis intersecting this point did it begin to make sense. A petroglyph panel not far away also added some clues to its function. After pondering the whole scene for some time, the answer finally became clear. This long central axis that ties the West Gap Narrows to the East Fremont villages is the lateral central division line of not only the temple center layout in the west basin, but also represents its central calendar ritual azimuth that splits the year along the summer cross-quarter shift axis and 260-day calendar axis, as viewed from Cairns B1 and B2 which are on and very near this line (see topographic map (Fig. 15:1). The ancient Tewa peoples of New Mexico used Geo-form stones in this same way (Ortiz 1973: 20).

How the Tewa Came to Sacred Mountains
They lived down below this world
In another world that was under a lake,
And gods lived with them there,
And animals and birds.
All of them spoke one language.
It was Tewa.

The world up here was a hazy, misty place,
still mud, too soft for people to walk on.

Down below, the people waited
For this world to harden.

When that time came,
They sent four pairs of messengers
Up through the lake to scout around
And see what it was like.
And right away, they saw four great mountains
Holding up the sky,
Four great sacred mountains shining
In the four directions,
Marking the boundaries of that world.

The mountain to the north was turquoise blue.
To the west, yellow,
To the south, red,
And to the sunrise it was white.

Other mountains marked the fifth direction—up,
And the sixth direction—down,
And the center of the world—
Exactly where the people stood.

Byrd Baylor, The Way to Make Perfect Mountains—
Native American Legends of Sacred Mountains (1997: 8)

Reprinted with permission from Cinco Puntos Press. From "The Way to Make Perfect Mountains" by Byrd Baylor (1979), Cinco Puntos Press. www.cincopuntos.com

Epilogue

A Prayer

O Great Father of our spirits—who's voice we hear in the wind and who's breath gives life to the world—Hear Me! We love this land, we will remember the use of thy land is a privilege given to our fathers and can be lost.

O Great spirit, make my people good keepers of this thy land so that when life fades as the sunset—my people may come to thee without shame.

(Kohler 1989: IV)

Many choice experiences with wild life and nature while working at the Gap over the years have wed me to this place as my most favorite archaeology site in the world. It is not the man-made architectural wonders of the past that now impress me the most. It is the complete lack of them. It is the keen observations of the world and the heavens and the creative genius of ancient inhabitants that gave birth to this special place. It is the simplicity of the lives of these ancient people connected with their universe in ways that brought divine harmony to their lives. There is little evidence of human conflict here. There has been limited site vandalism over the 500-year Fremont history at the Gap. This speaks of their reverence for sacred space that has been lost in our "enlightened" modern world.

I return to the Gap several times a year, sometimes with no particular research objective, just to meditate. But I have never come here without learning, without making some new discovery that continues to draw me back. Much of the mystery of the lives of the people who lived here is lost, but so much is gained from their unique records that has enriched my life for good. I hope this experience is shared by each individual who reads this book and comes to the Gap to see and understand a sacred wilderness temple center of deep enduring antiquity. May it endure as part of the cultural heritage of our Native American peoples and continue to teach ours and future generations the beauty and way of peace reflected in the heavens and sculpted in nature's landscape and wilderness plants and wild life. Come and see and experience. Leave it unmarred for those who follow.

Parowan Gap Terms

Anthropomorphs	Humanoid like form
Azimuth	A measured sight line direction with a compass
Cairn	A pile of stones set up for an observation station or as a survey marker
Ceramic shards	Pieces of broken pottery
Chevron	V shaped stripes
Cosmology	Beliefs based on studying the earth and heavens; treating the Universe as an orderly, related system; the processes of nature and the relation of all it parts, i.e., harmony in astroomy relates to mathematics, geometry, measure (in time and space), music, art and architecture, etc.
Epigraphy	The study of ancient writings: inscriptions, hieroglyphs, petroglyphs, pictrographs
Equinox	The time when the sun's path crosses the equator, making night and day of equal length about March 21 (vernal equinox) and September 21–22 (autumnal equinox)
Ethnographic	The branch of anthropology [archaeology] dealing with the scientific description of individual cultures
Geoform	Artistic creations on the ground with rocks
Gnomon	Standing object, such as a tree or rock, used to mark the sun's shadow for a specific date
Heliacal rise	First appearance of Venus as Morning Star. It continues to rise each morning for about 8 months (243 days) in the 584 day Venus synodic cycle

Hieroglyphic Writing	Conventionalized pictographic script or symbols designed to be read
Hierophany	Astronomical phenomenon in which structures, monuments or natural objects interact with specific sun, moon or star events on key cycle dates
Humanoids	In the form of a human
Leap Year	A day added in the calendar every 4 years to keep the horizon solar calendar aligned with solstices (fixed horizon dates)
Lithic scatter	Chipping debris from tool making
Lunar	Moon cycles, especially 4 moon phases: new moon, 1st half-moon, full moon, 2nd half-moon
Mano, Metate	Grinding stones used to grind seeds for food
Metonic Cycle	19 year moon/sun Conjunction cycle; a 5th century B.C. Greek astronomer named Meton found that the sun and moon have a same day "conjunction" every 19 years; the moon cycle's 235 lunations divided by 12 each year = approximately 19 years (moon 235 × 29.5 = 6,939 days or 19 years; sun 365.2 × 19 = 6,939 days or 19 years)
Numic	Uto-Aztecan language of Ute, Paiute, Goshute, Shoshone and Hopi
Petroglyph	"Symbols made upon a rock by pecking, incising, abrading or scratching" (Martineau 1973: 195)
Pictograph	"Picture writing in a painted form upon any material. Also, a picture representing and expressing an idea" (Martineau 1973: 196)
Solstice, Solar Transit	Sun's horizontal movement along horizon between its north summer solstice June 21, and south winter solstice December 21
Strata	In geology, a distinct bed of sedimentary rock deposited anciently
Symbol	"Any depiction or drawing used in pictography to convey any type of meaning. One of the characters, combinations, incorporations, or units of pictography" (Martineau 1973: 196)

Symbol Extension	"Additional and related meanings naturally derived from or suggested by the basic concept of a symbol" (Martineau 1973: 196)
Underworld	The winter is the underworld time of the year
Vision Quest Site	A secluded place on hills or mountains considered sacred; anciently small rock enclosures were built which often oriented a worshipper to a solstice, equinox, etc.; horizon point
Zoomorphs	Animal-like figures etched in stone as petroglyphs

Appendix

Ancient Native American Timeline
Parowan Gap–Present Day

Historic activity in the Parowan Gap following Mormon settlement is limited to transportation, ranching and grazing, water control, tree harvest for fencing, mineral exploration, hunting, and recreational activities. A coal mining operation located near the center of the Parowan Gap was short lived due to the poor quality and limited supply. The northeast flank of the Gap Narrows served as a stone quarry in the 1930s to build a wall around the Parowan cemetery.

Mormon Settlements (1849–Present)

Mormon Settlements in Southern Utah brought much contact and trade with Europeans. Some Indian tribes trapped beaver and traded pelts and horses with Spanish Colonies in California. Mormon settlers in Southern Utah reported that some of the Utes spoke Spanish. Throughout the last half of the 19th century, settlers continued to displace indigenous Numic-speaking peoples, and by 1890, ancient lifeways were no longer practiced by the Native Americans.

1849	Parley P. Pratt and 50 others made an expedition to Southern Utah to link Mormon settlements with California.
1851	167 people settled at Parowan; Iron Mission mining opened in Cedar City; Parowan was the hub of other Mormon settlements in Southern Utah from 1850 through the 1860s.
1853	Flooding in southern Utah; harsh winters
1856	Grasshopper plague

1850s–1860s	Indian Wars (Walker War 1853–54; Black Hawk War 1865–67)
	Mormons defended Paiutes against Navajo slave raids.
	Paiutes helped early settlements on the Virgin River at St. George with agriculture (corn, beans and squash) and home construction.

Spanish Exploration (1600–1847)

Spanish Explorers traveled north from settlements in Mexico, established a colony at what is now Sante Fe, New Mexico, and some colonies in what is now Arizona. This was the first European contact with Utes, Paiutes and other Numic peoples. Horses brought by the Spanish increased the Indian's hunting and gathering efficiency (also helped Utes raid neighboring tribes to capture slaves needed to trade with the Spanish).

Spanish expeditions typically engaged Indians as guides and interpreters. According to historian Pedro de Castenada, Coronado's expedition had 800 Aztec attendants. In 1604, an exploratory expedition sent by Juan de Onate met an Indian, probably a Southern Paiute who came from the north and spoke the Mexican (Uto-Aztecan) language.

1776	Escalante identified the Utah Lake Valley as an ideal location to establish a Spanish mission. He wrote of the first accounts of the lifeways of the Ute and Paiute peoples living in the area.
1776–1777	Dominguez-Escalante expedition established the Sante Fe Trail which passed through Cedar Valley and Parowan Valley. Later this became the Old Spanish Trail traveled by Jedediah Smith and John C. Fremont to California.
1817	Spanish expeditions came from Sante Fe to Utah Lake to trade with Timpanogos Utes for beaver pelts.
1821–1844	About 80 wagons and 150 men used the Spanish Trail each year to transport goods to California to exchange for mules, furs, gold and silver with an annual value of $130,000 (*World Book Encyclopedia*, 1963).

1825	Etienne Provost, Peter Ogden and Wm. Ashley trapped beaver in Utah.
1680	Pueblo Revolt August 13, (secretly organized against oppressive Spaniards). This date is the Sacred 260–105 Mesoamerican calendar New Year among Pueblo tribes and is the base date of the Mesoamerican calendar.
1604	Utah Lake region was thought by Spaniards to be a legendary lost city with gold.
1598	Mexico territorial expansion officially moved into what is now Utah, Colorado, Idaho and Wyoming.
1583	Antonio de Espejo in search of gold and silver has contact with Hopi's and Zuni's.
1540	Francisco Vasquez de Coronado and Spanish expeditions discover Hopi's and Zuni's in regions bordering Mexican territories.

Numic (Ute, Paiute, Goshute, Shoshone)

A.D. 1200–21st Century

Numic (Ute, Paiute, Goshute, Shoshone) Paiutes first lived by the sea, then crossed the west desert toward the rising sun at the red mountains—directed by their gods Tobats and Shinob; Northern Plains Indians also moved to the Great Basin in loosely organized family units.

Eastern Ute and Shoshoni adopted Plains tepee covered with hide and a conical shaped brush hut for a sweathouse, typical of the southern Utah Paiute wickiup.

Southern Paiutes had large well kept gardens adopted from neighboring Anasazi.

Food: seasonal hunting for big game; nets for "rabbit drives," bone harpoon and weir for fishing.

Shamans practiced "vision quest" solitary prayer vigils like the Plains Indians.

	Mythic tales and ritual life cycle from birth to death; burials were in rock crevices or caves.
A.D. 1200– Era of Drought (Tree Ring Dating)	Fremont decline and disappearance; gradual migration of Numic tribes to the Great Basin from neighboring areas.
A.D. 1064–1250	Sunset Crater volcanic eruption plus 60 other cinder cones.

Toltec of Ancient Mexico

A.D. 900–1200	Ancient Toltec from central Mexico had trade routes to turquoise mines near what is today, Elko, Nevada (Trace Analysis links ancient Mexican turquoise jewelry to ancient mines in Northern Nevada); evidences indicate that Toltec trails may have gone through Parowan Gap (260–105 day Sacred Mesoamerican calendar).

Fremont

A.D. 400–1300	The Fremont, the uniquely Utahn Native American culture, developed after transmission of technological complexes came across the Southwest from Mexico; the southern Anasazi and Utah Fremont cultures are quite comparable. They had:

- ◆ Clay pottery and figures, moccasins, stone balls, trough metates
- ◆ Permanent housing in dugout-pit earthen structures with wood and mud "roof" covers (oriented to solstices in Late Fremont period)
- ◆ Horticulture and Cultivation of frost and drought-resistant maize; squash, beans

Fremont culture has three subphases:

Late Fremont (Formative A.D. 900–1350)

- Rapid population increase, storage units and deeper pit dwellings
- Larger adobe buildings were oriented toward solstices
- Corrugated pottery, painted wares
- Arrowhead point types for hunting; bone tools and harpoon-points were used for extensive domestic and economic activities

Middle Fremont (Formative A.D. 750–900)

The larger population had nuclear household habitation "rancherias" for clans

- Dwellings—shallow oval pits, or stone masonry buildings, cliff granaries
- Early pottery graywares; metate trough, bone and stone tools
- Beads, awls, needles, figurines, moccasin, basketry, and stone balls

Early Fremont (Formative A.D. 100–750)
= Pueblo Basketmaker II

Primarily hunting-gathering; horticulture in some areas

- Shallow, round pithouses were built with external work areas in small settlements of 1–3 structures; clustering of sites
- Lithic arrowheads made for bow and arrow hunting
- Pottery introduced; temporary food storage occurred

Archaic

6,300 B.C.–A.D. 400

The Desert Archaic culture was in the Great Basin

+ Hunting food—mountain sheep, mule deer, elk, antelope, bison, rabbit, beaver, water fowl, birds, and rodents. Large lanceolate-type arrowheads used.

+ Floral gathering—wheatgrass, pickleweed, Indian ricegrass, prickly pear cactus, rabbit brush, sagebrush, saltbrush, blackberry, chokecherry, onion, pinyon.

+ Fiber items—nets, baskets, cord, and snares. Figurines of animals and humans.

+ Dwellings—flexible, highly-adaptive nomadic way of life (a universal characteristic)

Four subphases of Northern Colorado plateau Desert Archaic (Schroedl 1976):

Dirty Devil (1300 B.C.–A.D. 500)

Gypsum point, corn, bow and arrow, pit structures, bell-shaped storage pits at end of phase

Green River (2500 B.C.–1300 B.C.)

Gypsum point, triangular corner-notched arrow points; food—mountain sheep and amaranths

Castle Valley (4200 B.C.–2500 B.C.)

Greater reliance on grasses and forbs; late addition of slab lined fire pits and arrow points

Black Knoll (6300 B.C.–4200 B.C.)

Pinto and Northern side-notched points; emphasis on big game hunting, plus gathering of cactus, amaranth and chenopods; grinding implements used

Neighboring Pueblo Anasazi

Southwestern Pueblo Anasazi cultures border the Colorado Plateau on the south and have overlapping cultural boundaries with evidence of Anasazi influence into Utah. Berry's (1975: 78–80) summary data on the Kayenta and Mesa Verde Anasazi data is listed here as a research framework in the Southwest. (B.P. = Before Present)

Pueblo V	250 B.P.–present
Pueblo IV (Towns)	650–250 B.P.
Pueblo III (Villages)	850–650 B.P.
Pueblo II (Kiva)	1050–850 B.P.
Pueblo I (Bow and Arrow)	1200–1050 B.P.
Basketmaker III	1500–1200 B.P.
Basketmaker II	1950–1450 B.P.
Basketmaker I	Pre-1950 B.P.

Calendar Petroglyph at Sheep Wash, Uintah Basin

While the seasonal calendar cycles of the sun, moon, and stars based on latitude are universal and constant the world over, the way people observed and recorded time in different places, cultures and ages is diverse. Divisions of time and New Year dates vary widely. New Years fits most naturally near a solstice or equinox. My discovery of the first solar petroglyph markers for solstice and equinox in Utah in the Uintah Basin in 1980 shows the basic primitive calendar for marking the season quarters.

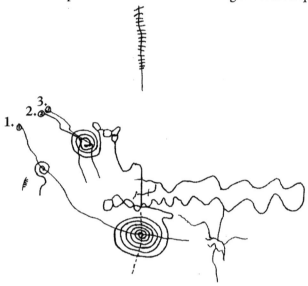

- ✦ Numbered lines 1,2,3 are equinox-rise shadow progressions.
- ✦ Vertical dotted line bisecting the large spiral indicates the winter solstice sunset shadow.
- ✦ Horizontal squiggly line has 15 turns to the right return (day-count to full moon?)
- ✦ 4 circles at end of both spirals suggest 4 seasons created by solstices and equinoxes.

The simple universal way to divide the year is by halving along the natural 4-quarter lines based on the solar transit solstice extremes and its mid-equinox point. On a horizon calendar, the sun appears to move back and forth in a fixed number of days between its northern and southern extremes that determines the seasons because of the temperature changes from the sun's passage across the sky at a higher or lower angle as the earth tilts on its axis. Without this constant axis "wobble", life as we know it on earth could not exist. Whether or not the ancients understood this cause and effect does not matter. They recorded what they saw in the movements in the heavens that affected their life cycles.

Bibliography

Aveni, Anthony F.
1980   *Skywatchers of Ancient Mexico.* University of Texas Press, Austin, Texas.
1997   *Stairways to the Stars.* Skywatching in Three Great Ancient Civilizations. John Wiley and Sons, Inc. New York.

Baylor, Byrd
1997   *The Way to Make Perfect Mountains.* Native American Legends of Sacred Mountains. Cinco Punto Press, El Paso, Texas.

Bunte, Pamela A., and Franklin, Robert J.
1990   *The Paiute.* Franklin W. Porter III—General Editor. Chelsea House Publishers, N.Y., Philadelphia.

Hadingham, Evan
1985   *Early Man and the Cosmos.* University of Oklahoma Press, Norman, Oklahoma.

Harbottle, Garman, and Weigand, Phil C.
1992   Turquoise in Pre-Columbian America. *Scientific American.* 266 (2): 78–85, February.

Jones, David M. and Molyneaux, Brian L.
2002   *The Mythology of the Americas.* Anness Publishing Limited, London.

Kohler, Kenneth Olsen
1989   *Other Truths Not Guessed: The Story of the Sevier Fremont Indian.* Classic Printing Co., St. George, Utah.

La Farge, Oliver
1957   *Laughing Boy.* Houghton Mifflin Company, Boston.

Malmstrom, Vincent H.
1997   *Cycles of the Sun, Mysteries of the Moon.* University of Texas Press, Austin.

Martineau, La Van

1994   *The Rocks Begin to Speak*. KC Publications, Inc. Las Vegas, Nevada.

1998   *Southern Paiutes; Legends, Lore, Language, and Lineage*. KC Publications, Inc. Las Vegas, Nevada.

Matheson, Alva

1990   *Indian Stories and Legends*. Southern Utah State College Media Service, Cedar City, Utah.

Meighan, Clement W., Norman E. Coles, Frank D. Davis, Geraldine M. Greenwood, William M. Harrison, and E. Heath MacBain.

1956   Archeological Excavations in Iron County, Utah. *Anthropological Papers*, No. 25, University of Utah, Salt Lake City.

Morris, Nowell L.

1998   The Parowan Gap Archaeoastronomy Report; Space, Time, Light and Number. Produced from ARCON contract preliminary draft report (unedited) by author for private publication. Solarnetics Inc., Salt Lake City.

Moore, Patrick

1968   *Amateur Astronomy*, W. W. Norton and Company, Inc. New York.

Norman, V. Garth

1973   Izapa Sculpture, Part 1: Album, *Papers of the New World Archaeological Foundation*, No. 30, Provo.

1976   Izapa Sculpture, Part 2: Text, *Papers of the New World Archaeological Foundation*, No. 30, Provo.

1980a   Astronomical Orientations of Izapa Sculptures, MS Thesis. Department Of Anthropology, Brigham Young University.

1980b   A Theoretical Approach to Identifying and Interpreting Calendrical Petroglyphs in Utah. *Utah Rock Art*, Vol. 4. Utah Rock Art Research Association, Salt Lake City, 1985, Paper presented at First URARA Annual Symposium, 1980.

1980c   Identifying Solstice and Equinox Petroglyphs in Northeastern Utah and their Cultural Relations. *Utah Rock Art*, Vol. 4. Utah Rock Art Research Association, Salt Lake City, 1985. Paper presented at the Great Basin Conference, 1980, and at first Annual URARA Symposium, 1980.

1981   A Winter Solstice Sun Watch Station at Petroglyph Panel P–17 in Dry Fork Ashley Valley, Uintah basin; Developing a Methodology for Interpreting Selected Rock Art. *Utah Rock Art*, Vol. 4. Utah Rock Art Research Association, Salt Lake City, 1985. Paper presented at the Second Annual URARA Symposium, 1981.

1982   An Equinox Watch Station in Cottonwood Canyon as a Possible Marker for Annual Spring Hunting Ritual. *Utah Rock Art*, Vol. 4. Utah Rock

Art Research Association, Salt Lake City, 1985. Paper presented at 1982 Annual URARA symposium.

1990   An Equinox Solar Movie Ritual Hunting Panel in Dry Fork, Utah.

1991   A Hunting Jump Site Narrative Linear Panel in Capitol Reef.

1992   Legless Big Horn Sheep of Capitol Reef. Unpublished paper presented at the Annual URARA Symposium, September, 1992.

1994   *Data Recovery Plan for Parowan Gap/Parowan Valley Archaeological District, Iron county, Utah.* State ISTEA Enhancements Project Proposal. Archaeological Research Consultants (ARCON), American Fork, Utah. Ms. on file, and at Iron County Commission Office, Parowan, Utah.

2002a   *Parowan Gap Archaeological Project, Volume One: Field Report: Cultural Resources Evaluation of Proposed Phase 1 Construction.* Research Report No. 2002–1. Archaeological Research Consultants (ARCON), American Fork, Utah.

2002b   *Parowan Gap Archaeological Project, Volume Two: Rock Art Catalogue.* Research Report No. 2002–2. Archaeological Research Consultants (ARCON), American Fork, Utah.

2002c   *Parowan Gap Archaeological Project Interpretive Report.* Research Report No. 2002–4. (ARCON) American Fork, Utah.

Ortiz, Alfonso

1973   *The Tewa World: Space, Time, Being and Becoming in a Pueblo Society.* The University of Chicago Press, Chicago.

Palmer, William R.

1946   *Paiute Indian Legends.* (Private publication republished in 1957 with new title).

1957   *Why the North Star Stands Still.* Prentice Hall, Inc., Englewood Cliffs, New Jersey.

1978   *Why the North Star Stands Still; and other Indian Legends.* Zion Natural History Association, Springdale, Utah.

Riley, C. L.

1986   An Overview of the Greater Southwest in the Protohistoric Period. In *Ripples in the Chichimec Sea. New Considerations of Southwestern-Mesoamerican Interactions,* edited by F. J. Mathien and R.H. McGuire, 45–54. Southern Illinois University Press, Carbondale and Edwardsville.

Smith, Anne M.

1993   *Shoshone Tales.* University of Utah Press, Salt Lake City, Utah.

Tedlock, Barbara

1983   *Time and the Highland Maya.* University of New Mexico Press, Albuquerque.

Thompson, J. Eric S.
1960   *Maya Hieroglyphic Writing: An Introduction.* University of Oklahoma Press, Norman, Oklahoma.

Toll, Roger
2005   The Four Corners, Going back in time on Native American Land, *Sky Magazine.*

Trejo, Judy
1997   *Circle Dance Songs of the Paiute and Shoshone.* Canyon Records Production, Phoenix, Arizona.

Wauchope, Robert and Willey, Gordon
1965   *Handbook of Middle American Indians Volume Three, Archaeology of Southern Mesoamerica Part Two.* University of Texas, Austin.

Waters, Frank
1963   *Book of the Hopi,* New York: The Viking Press.

Widdison, Jerold G. Editor
1991   *The Anasazi; Why did they leave? Where did they go?* Anasazi Heritage Center, Dolores, Colorado. Panel discussion sponsored by the Bureau of Land Management as part of the "Four Corners Tribute," June 19, 1990. Discussants: James Judge, David Breternitz, Linda Cordell, George Gumerman, Leigh Jenkins, Edmund Ladd, and William Lipe.

About the Author ——————

V. Garth Norman

Archaeologist/Epigrapher/Archaeoastonomer

V. Garth Norman has researched antiquities in Mesoamerica and Western North America for over 40 years. He began researching Utah rock art during archaeological surveys in 1977, after completing a 12-year pre-Mayan Izapa Sculpture study in southern Mexico for the New World Archaeological Foundation's Izapa Project in 1976. That work, along with his Astronomical Orientations of Izapa Sculpture thesis (1980), provided the foundation for exploring Utah rock art.

    Norman discovered the first sun-oriented and shadow-calendar petroglyphs in Utah at three sites in the Book Cliffs and Uintah Basin, and reported at the Great

Basin Conference in 1980 ("Identifying Solstice and Equinox Petroglyphs in North-eastern Utah and Their Cultural Relations"). Norman introduced his rock art solar calendar research method the same year to the Utah Rock Art Research Association with positive results. He researched and documented numerous other calendar petro-glyph and observatory promontory sites across the Colorado Plateau over the next decade before starting the Parowan Gap project in 1993.

Norman has Graduate Degrees in Ancient Studies and in Archaeology-Anthropology from Brigham Young University. He has traveled and researched widely and participated in numerous professional archaeological symposiums in the USA, Canada, Mexico, and Europe, including Cambridge, Harvard, University of Maryland, University of Texas, and the National University of Mexico. He has affiliated with the Society for American Archaeology (SAA), the American Anthropological Association (AAA), the International Congress of Americanists, the Utah Professional Archaeo-logical Council (UPAC), and the Utah Rock Art Research Association.

Norman has been director and owner of Archaeological Research Consultants (ARCON) since 1982 and has authored numerous Cultural Resources inventory reports. He is president of the Ancient America Foundation for professional archae-ological research of historic sites and antiquities of particular interest to the LDS (Mormon) community. He and his wife, Cheryl, reside in American Fork, Utah, and have three married daughters and fourteen grandchildren.

Archaeologist Garth Norman has crafted a truly brilliant treatise on what is emerging as perhaps the most phenomenal wilderness temple center and calendar observatory in the Americas. Functioning with utter precision for over 4000 years, this magnificent 260-day and 105-day calendar clock allowed tribal shamans to remain synchronously attuned to the rhythms of nature's seasonal periods of conception, gestation, birth, and development. Illustrated by art historian Lance Harding, this work carefully documents the nearly 100 petroglyph panels, numerous figures, strategically positioned sunrise and sunset observation cairns, and the remains of a prehistoric cave excavated by Norman. Written with the precision and detail of a master archaeologist, *The Parowan Gap: Nature's Perfect Observatory*, serves as a self-guided tour for anyone who wants to visit what is presently one of North America's best kept secrets. Definitely an archaeo-astronomical wonderland: highly recommended.

Scott Olsen, Ph.D.
Author of *The Golden Section: Nature's Greatest Secret*

Garth Norman's introduction and self-guided interpretive tour of the Parowan Gap is indispensable for any scholar, student or amateur interest in North American archaeology and rock art. After having experienced the Parowan Gap firsthand, while participating in the ARCON archaeology project over the past ten years, I have come to know that it is one of the most important ancient sites in all of North America. After recording its vast amount of intriguing petroglyphs, and assisting with the survey documentation of its calendar observatory sites, I am convinced that the wealth of knowledge at the Gap is unsurpassed by any other archaeological site anywhere in the Western United States. Its naturally observable astronomical markers, and sun, moon and star signs open up the minds of the ancient Native Americans to us in an extent and depth never believed possible. Norman has also found the Gap to be a natural temple center where God, man, and nature co-exist in harmony at one location— "God's own House" on earth for "Man," as Ute chief Wakara told early pionerr settlers.

C. Lance Harding, Ph.D.
from The Prince's School of Traditional Arts, London;
Member of Kairos—a foundation for the recovery of
traditional values in art and science